BY ANDREW TOBIAS

Money Angles
The Invisible Bankers
Getting By on $100,000 a Year (and Other Sad Tales)
The Only Investment Guide You'll Ever Need
Fire and Ice
The Funny Money Game

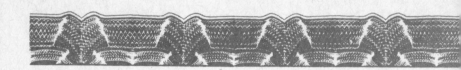

MONEY

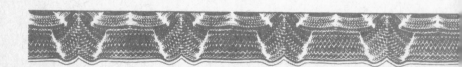

ANGLES

by Andrew Tobias

LINDEN PRESS / SIMON & SCHUSTER
NEW YORK 1984

3 5 7 9 10 8 6 4

The material in this book has originally appeared in *Playboy*,
The American Lawyer, *Parade*, *Esquire*, *Fortune*, *Savvy*, *TV Guide*,
The New York Times Book Review, and *The New York Times Magazine*,
in slightly different form.

Library of Congress Cataloging in Publication Data

Tobias, Andrew P.
Money angles.
Includes index.
1. Investments.   2. Finance, Personal.   I. Title.
HG4521.T59   1984   332.024   84-15762
ISBN 0-671-50804-0

For L. P.

Contents

SOURCES OF WEALTH

SOURCES OF WISDOM

SOURCES OF WEALTH

Propagandists, from Shakespeare to Jacqueline Susann, have been telling the unrich that money doesn't buy happiness. The unrich, not being immune to spasms of common sense, sometimes wonder about this.

—Anthony Haden-Guest

1

FINANCIAL FOREPLAY
Why All This Interest in Getting Rich?

Money, it's often been said, won't buy happiness. *This is a myth.*

I mean, come on!

But there is an element of truth to even the tritest saying, and the fact is that money will reliably buy happiness only for those who don't have it. *Getting* money brings happiness; having it may or may not.

Several of the chapters that follow are about getting rich. Getting rich slowly, getting rich with fancy footwork, getting rich quick. But what's this preoccupation with getting rich at all? Just how much fun is it—really—to be rich?

(Hint: How much fun is it to be great-looking?)

Here are the advantages of being rich: you don't have to take the subway, you don't have to clean your bathroom, you don't have to wait until after eleven to call. Here are the disadvantages: taxes, accountants, guilt and the persistent fear that you will somehow lose your money and be reduced to taking the subway, cleaning your bathroom and waiting until after eleven to call. (Also, truly incredible amounts of junk mail.)

But this is the crucial point: There is a world of difference between cleaning your toilet when you have always cleaned it and cleaning it after years of having had someone clean it for you. There is a world of difference between living in a smallish apartment on the second floor and living in a smallish apartment on the second floor after you've lived in a biggish apartment with a view.

It's which way you're headed that counts, not how much you've got.

Consider two families, one making $75,000 a year but knowing, somehow, that its income will be falling to $40,000; the other making $15,000 a year but assured of an increase to $25,000. I submit that the family getting by on $15,000 a year, with its eye on $25,000, is likely to be happier than the $75,000-a-year family facing $40,000.

One family is earning a fifth as much as the other, yet it is likely to be happier. Why? Because things are looking up.

This, indeed, is one of the things that make inflation so pleasant in its early stages, before folks catch on. Almost everybody feels he's doing a little better. Wages are rising, home prices are rising, profits are rising—and at first, nobody pays much attention to the fact that prices are rising, too, so the gains are illusory. (In fact, in the early stages, they may not be. The prosperous feeling inflation at first brings can bolster confidence and stimulate growth.)

It's also one of the pluses of growing older. Your income is likely to rise gradually with seniority. Even if it doesn't, your standard of living can improve every year. That is because a toaster oven, once acquired, need not be reacquired each year. Gradually, even without a rise in real income, you may find yourself with a growing pile of household appliances, a larger and larger savings account, a cozier and cozier life. (Or you may squander it all.)

A lot of the inequality in the world is inequality based simply on age—and is, thus, inequality of the least offensive kind. A kid fresh out of college—even Harvard—is likely to own nothing but some books, clothes and a stereo, while a postal worker who has been careful may have $75,000 stashed away by the time he retires, plus his home free and clear (plus his generous government pension). And that is undoubtedly a good thing. Bad enough that, physically, we should decline steadily after the age of twenty-five, or whenever it is—wouldn't it be depressing if we also started out rich and grew progressively poorer?

I had $400,000 worth of stock options when I was twenty-one, but was fortunately too busy to spend any of it. The president of the company ultimately went to jail for the enthusiasm of his bookkeeping, and my options wound up worthless. Because the paper fortune had never seemed quite real to me (well, it wasn't real, as it turned out), I didn't particularly miss it. But others in the company had easily secured loans against their impending bonanzas—surely the stock couldn't drop 90 percent in six months, they and their bankers had reasoned; oh, but it could! it could!—and had begun living like the millionaires they would doubtless soon be. But weren't.

Even if our ship had not foundered, they were sailing too fast, in my view. For if you have a Lear jet when you're in your early thirties, as the president of the company did, what sort of toys have you to look forward to when you're forty or fifty? A yacht? A castle on the Potomac? He had those, too.

A director friend of mine who really did make a small fortune at an absurdly early age, and not just on paper, understood the importance of pacing. Rather than immediately rising to the Jaguar and Bel Air style he could have afforded, but not necessarily maintained or improved upon, he put most of his money to work for the future and allowed himself a pleasant succession of indulgences. It was a decade before he finally sprang for the house with the spectacular view, and there is still some question about putting in a pool. Every year, life gets a little better.

In broad form, here are the possibilities:

You can start out with nothing to speak of and get nothing to speak of—drab. You can start out with nothing to speak of but gradually get more—satisfying. You can make a pile and lose it, as I've described. You can make a pile and keep it, which has got to be kind of fun (one self-made friend of mine, thirty-six, has, as a footnote to his grander extravagances, a weekly $50 Oriental bone massage; money manager Dean LeBaron is reported to have owned a working flight simulator and an electric driveway that melts snow). Or you can have great wealth handed to you at birth. Not so surprisingly, that last is a decidedly mixed blessing. It can rob you of your sense of purpose; it can instill no small measure of guilt.

I know a man who had the misfortune to inherit $1 million when he was three. (His grandfather was a minor oil titan.) He is exceptionally talented, superbly schooled and, fundamentally, a mess. In truth, he's less of a mess now that, at forty-one, he has finally come into his own (though his father still manages his money). But his better frame of mind has little to do with his wealth; it's his professional and civic successes that have saved him. And yet, even now, when he stops long enough to stare into his vodka martini, he is, at root, unhappy.

One day not long ago, he told me—with no small sense of pride—that after nearly a year, he had finally opened up to the new shrink he'd begun seeing. (If I were paying somebody $85 an hour, I'd try to get it all on the table in the first half hour.) He had been holding back, he said, but had now just put it all out there. *Everything.* Whereupon he enumerated a list of miseries and peculiarities with which I had long since become familiar.

"What about your main problem?" I asked him.

"What main problem?" he answered.

"Your money! Surely, you've talked to your shrink about that."

"My money is not a problem!" he shouted. *"Why do you keep bringing it up?"*

In nearly a year with his new shrink, my friend had never mentioned that he was rich. Or that his dad managed his affairs and saw all the checks he wrote. Or that many of his friendships over the years had broken up over his suspicion that people liked him only for his money.

He hadn't mentioned it, he finally lied, because he was afraid the shrink would up his fee. But the real reason he hadn't mentioned it was that it was too personal and painful. The stuff about the carrots and the brassieres and his ex-wife was *easy* to talk about, by comparison.

And then there's my friend whose ancestor had been given much of Long Island by King George. The wealth into which he was born was such that as a child, where you or I might have knocked a porcelain figurine off the coffee table, he had once scribbled in crayon in a Gutenberg Bible, or so he claims. Anyway, this fine fellow has wallowed much of his adult life in the kind of aimless depression only Woody Allen has the skill to portray. Alone in a huge house except for the staff; jetting off to be alone in another huge house except for the staff—sad.

But if it is a problem to be born rich, consider the problem of having a fortune fall on your head in midlife, as it does when you win the lottery or when Michael Anthony shows up at your door with an anonymous gift of $1 million. What a discombobulation that is! Some handle it well ("Try *me*! Try *me*!" I hear you cry), others less so.

Ken Proxmire had been earning $15,000 a year in Detroit when in 1977 he won the Michigan lottery. He went bankrupt five years later. It seems that his first move upon winning was to quit his job and that his second was to transplant his family from Detroit to Fresno, California, where he bought a new house and a new car and started picking up the tab when he went out with friends. It was, in his words, "a big ego trip."

He wanted to start a bowling alley, but couldn't find a bank willing to lend him $500,000 against his annual $50,000 lottery winnings. So instead he bought a pool hall and later began selling pool tables at three locations. He moved his two brothers and their families out from Michigan to work in the business, but a failing economy and high interest rates killed off the pool-table market, leaving him with $60,000 in debts, three households to support and no income but his lottery winnings. He filed for bankruptcy in 1982 and told the *New York Times* that it was such a bad experience he was planning to write a book of advice for other lottery winners. (Now, there's a big market.)

You can have problems no matter how much money you've got. In fact, the more you've got, the richer your mix of problems.

I was once a minor speaker at a Young Presidents Organization meeting in Munich. It was a meeting of men and their wives —mostly Americans—who had attained corporate presidencies before the age of forty and had flown to Munich to further their executive educations.

Three of the most popular talks at the university, as the tax-deductible week was called, were "Acupuncture," "Passive Men, Wild Women" and "How to Make Health Food Taste Good." A talk on the Soviet energy situation and its impact on the world economy, offered by the Harvard professor most often quoted on such subjects, drew eighteen people to a room set up for five hundred.

I was not a big hit at that multimillion-dollar confab, because my talk, "Getting By on $100,000 a Year," was meant mostly to be funny, whereas these folks, facing a bad economy (not that they were likely ever to be reduced to *so* little), came expecting some hard, money-scrimping advice.

One of the major speakers (or "resources," as Y.P.O. calls its faculty) was C. Northcote Parkinson. You've heard of Parkinson's laws? Parkinson, at seventy-three, was magnificent— ever so slow but ever so British, ever so classy. Even watching him ascend the podium—no brief spectacle—was engaging. Picture Alfred Hitchcock in the role.

"I have been asked to talk to you today," Parkinson said

slowly, "on the subject of Parkinson's . . . laws." (Drop your voice a half octave and tuck down your chin on "laws.") "I suppose," he said, "I am as qualified as anyone to address this subject."

But, he said, before speaking about Parkinson's six laws, he wanted to tell us that he had, just the day before—at this very meeting place, gazing out upon this very audience—formulated his *seventh . . .* law. (Drop your voice, tuck your chin.)

I need hardly tell you that the members of the audience were rapt, edging forward on their chairs to attend the christening of Parkinson's seventh law, even if, in truth, the only one of the first six they remembered was the one about work expanding to fill the time allotted to it.

"Parkinson's seventh . . . law," said Parkinson, "holds that *the ablest men*" . . . pause . . . "*get the prettiest girls.*"

The woman to my right, a total stranger, very beautiful, very Neiman-Marcus, perhaps thirty-six, turned to me and whispered loudly, "Yeah—and when they hit forty, they get *dumped.*"

My eyes widened and I stuttered reassuringly—it was all I could think of—"Oh, I'm sure that's not true."

"You bet your sweet ass it is, honey," she replied.

Parkinson went on about his business. But the point of this, none too swift in coming, is that I have myself, without even so much as querying the great man for permission, formulated Parkinson's *eighth . . .* law. And, for that matter, his ninth.

Parkinson's eighth law states, or should, that *expenses expand to the cash plus credit available.*

Or: Whatever you've got, you spend a little more.

Or: Enough is never enough.

(Or, as the sign over the Lone Star Café has it: TOO MUCH IS NOT ENOUGH.)

Parkinson's ninth law: *A luxury once sampled becomes a necessity.*

You say you don't particularly mind not having remote-control TV? I can state with some certainty, in that case, that you've never had one. You don't mind having to jump in and out of bed every time you want to kill the sound or change the channel? I never minded, either.

Touch-Tone dialing, the six-minute baked potato, sea planes vaulting Friday afternoon traffic to the beach—those are things it's a cinch to be happy without before they've been invented; possible to be happy without even after they've been invented; but oh, so hard to be happy without once you've gotten used to them.

Pace yourself! *Tease* yourself with anticipation. *Ease* the fingers of your aspiration up the inner thigh of your cupidity. Tickle your fancy.

Of *course* money buys happiness! But both will last longer if you remember the importance of foreplay.

2

THE BASICS
Buy Low, Sell High

Okay—let's get started. This is a book about money (let's not mince words), and there are certain things you simply must know before stepping out of the house even that very first time, aged five-and-a-half, with 25 cents in your pocket and mischief on your mind. You are an economic entity, you are responsible for your own balance of payments, and there is no way you will accumulate the wealth we both know you deserve, short of some fortuitous inheritance, without your knowing the basics of personal finance.

Here they are:

1. Buy Low, Sell High. What *most* people do—particularly those who can least afford it—is to invest wistfully, buying whatever it is they *wish* they had bought sometime before. They are convinced this is the way to make money, because all the success stories are about people who have been making money this way (whatever "this way" happens to be at the time), and so finally they take the greedy plunge—and are the last ones into the pool.

Now, you say, how can "most people" be the last ones in? Surely this is a contradiction in terms. But it is not. The reason

95 percent of the people into some investment may be among the last ones in is that the other 5 percent, who got in first, have most of the money. It takes a lot of poor suckers, in at the end in $3,000 chunks, to enrich a few millionaires.

Certainly this is the way it works with pyramid schemes. I sell to 10 who sell to 100 who sell to 1,000 who sell to 10,000—at whatever level the music stops, as it always must, more folks will be in at the last level than at all previous levels combined.

But forget pyramids. What I really want to do here is tell you the story of my 5,000 silver dimes. These were dimes minted back in the days when the coin was actually worth more than the metal. I had bought half a bag of them—5,000 dimes—for $3,000 in 1979, not because I thought there really would be rioting in the streets and a total currency collapse, as so many of our newsletter writers were predicting, and certainly not because I had any idea what the Hunts were up to or had to make a lot of phone calls, but simply because it can never hurt to be careful.

With silver then selling around $9 an ounce, these dimes were not bought as an investment, they were bought as insurance. I put the bag away, planning never to look at it again. And then the prices of gold and silver quadrupled. According to the newspaper, my $3,000 insurance lode could be sold for $12,000-plus —not the sort of quick killing, I don't mind admitting, I'm accustomed to. (Unless, as has happened, I'm the one getting killed.)

I had planned never to look at that silver again (truth to tell, I had never even unsealed the bag, so trusting a soul am I—it could have been filled with emeralds for all I knew), but there was silver at $40-odd an ounce, and there was I in a rattling taxi with the unopened bag on my lap on my way down to Deak-Perera, on the second floor of 630 Fifth Avenue, Rockefeller Center, New York, New York, mulling over all the things that could go wrong. Because I am a firm believer that if a thing looks too good to be true, it probably is.

The most obvious snag—that I could be mugged on my way out of Deak-Perera by any of the scores of less fortunate souls who doubtless knew a good thing when they saw one, too— was not the one encountered. Instead, I arrived at Deak-Perera to find a pushing, shoving mob. Obviously, I had not been the only boy in New York to recognize a classic market top.

I am not the pushing, shoving type (never mind what my friends may tell you), and thus felt certain that if I even stayed to try to sell my silver, by the time my turn actually came Deak-Perera would have run out of cash. (For reasons I leave to your imagination, everyone seems to sell gold and silver for cash.) Or that the price, which was by then moving several dollars a day, would have come crashing back down to more reasonable levels.

But I discovered the most remarkable thing: of all the people crowded into that small room, only three of us were there to sell. Everyone else was there to buy.

Gold was peaking at an all-time high ($875 plus a hefty commission), but you should have seen the people lined up to buy even a single Krugerrand, most of them looking as though they could ill afford to (anyone who buys Krugerrands one at a time has, by definition, no business buying Krugerrands at all), but scraping up the cash all the same.

Before long, some of that cash was in my pocket. And months later, when the price of silver returned to around $8 an ounce, I ordered more dimes.

Buy low, sell high.

2. Diversify. Brave words, I know. Yet it's remarkable how many of us chickens manage inadvertently to have most of our eggs you know where.

Howard Ruff, of whom more in a later chapter, was on the "MacNeil-Lehrer Report" in 1981 after gold had fallen back from $875 the ounce to around $500.

"My advice," he said, "is if gold falls below four fifty, you can take maybe twenty-five percent of the money you have set aside and buy some; if it falls below four twenty-five, you take another twenty-five percent; and at four hundred you sell the kids, mortgage the farm, any other cliché you can think of" —and buy gold.

That's not what I'd call diversification.

I don't know where the price of gold is going; but I do know that no one else knows either.* In light of which, selling the kids and mortgaging the farm and betting all your money on one horse makes very little sense indeed. Even if gold had shot up to $2,000 (it fell to $297, and is today wherever the *Wall Street Journal* says it is), it would have been bad advice. The future is unknowable. It's foolish to bet everything on one scenario.

Diversify.

3. Never Invest in Anything that Eats or Needs Repairing. This is a line attributed to vaudevillian Billy Rose, who apparently was in some of the same tax shelters I am.

4. You Are Buying a Stock, Not a Company. Or perhaps you are buying neither. But if the stock market *is* your arena, and unless you are one of these mad multimillionaires out to buy not just a few thousand shares of Disney but the whole bloody thing, you are buying a stock, not a company.

Apple Computer: great company. Can anyone deny it? The stock went public at $22 a share. That doesn't sound like much for a great company. And up it shot, to 35. Even *that* doesn't

---

* That I know very little about where gold prices will go was amply demonstrated one night on a "Tonight Show" that had aired originally when gold was around $300, but that was being rerun when it was pushing $850. At first I couldn't figure out why this Best-of-Carson seemed so vividly familiar—gee, I thought, the first time around I must really have been paying attention— when suddenly Johnny announced that I would be the next guest. Now *there's* something to make you spill your milk and cookies all over the bed! Especially when you find yourself telling America, "Gee, Johnny—gold at three hundred dollars an ounce? I don't know—looks awfully risky to me!"

It *was* awfully risky, but nearly tripled all the same.

sound like much for a piece of the pie, but the first question any potential investor should have asked—and many didn't—was, how many pieces in the pie?

The Apple pie was divided into 52 million slices. At $35 each, the four-year-old company was selling for just under $2 billion —about 15 times sales, 150 times earnings.

So the first thing I did was short a few shares of Apple at $35, betting the price would fall, and then, like everyone else in the world, I went out to buy an Apple computer. The salesman, who was nineteen, showed me all its terrific features and I said it looked swell, not that I had any competence to judge, but that before I plunked down my four grand I kind of wanted to have a chance to talk to his supervisor. (I had been in business myself at nineteen, and I, too, had had trouble getting people to take me seriously.) No problem! A wave and a shout, and over came this kid's supervisor, who was—that's right—seventeen.

I know this because when I made some sort of off-hand remark about being short Apple stock, he allowed as to how I knew nothing about computers (true!) and had to be crazy, because Apple was nothing less than sensational. He had just put all his college money into the stock, he said. (That's how I knew he was seventeen—he was about to graduate from high school.)

"What did you pay for the stock?" I asked him.

"Thirty-five," he told me.

"Oh, God," I said, "you probably bought it from *me*. For heaven's sake, sell it before it goes much lower." It had already begun to slip.

He said I was crazy, Apple's a great company. I said, yes, Apple's a great company but at the present time it's a lousy stock. You're buying a stock, not a company, I told him. He showed me the Apple expansion modules (nodules? slits? something) that would allow them to cream the competition. I left, only to buy my Apple a few weeks later someplace else.

When the stock touched $25 I covered my short and pock-
eted my profit. If I had had any guts I would have waited a
while longer and pocketed a much bigger profit—it bottomed
out at 14¼. I fear that's where the young salesman sold out,
because that's where folks who buy at the top usually do.

Meanwhile, the flip side:

At 3½ in 1982—now 28—Chrysler was the iffiest of companies, but a great stock.

You are buying a stock, not a company. *

5. Beware the Permanent Trend. It was Montesquieu who
observed that the world's population was declining, and that if
the rate kept up, in ten centuries the earth would become a
desert. (Or perhaps "deserted"—translations of this complex-
ity can be tricky.) It is by this same reasoning that a fourteen-
year-old growing two inches a year can be expected by sixty to
be twelve foot four, and by which malpractice insurance premiums, among others, are set, but that's another story. The
point here is that nothing is forever. Not diamonds, not rising
oil prices, not inflation, not depression, not the steady appreciation of real estate, not even—are you ready?—the steady appreciation of real estate in Beverly Hills.

6. When Flying to London, Book through to Prague. The way
this was working recently, it actually cost more to fly to London
on the Concorde than to fly there on the Concorde, switch
planes, and fly on to Prague. (There was a similar gimmick with

---

* Wells Fargo Bank runs what's known as an index fund. It buys shares in
virtually all the stocks in the Standard & Poor's 500 in order to guarantee a
performance that almost precisely mirrors that index. The only judgmental act
the fund performs is to weed out those few stocks that are of *such* poor quality
as to defy even the most minimal fiduciary standards. The real garbage. In
1976, there were nineteen such outcasts. The Institute for Econometric Research, which publishes *Market Logic,* decided to keep track of those nineteen. Seven years later they had climbed 277 percent, a gain four times that of
the S&P 500.

Paris and Budapest.) So what some frugal folk were doing was flying over to London on the Concorde and just throwing away the rest of the ticket.

Whether this particular opportunity remains imbedded in the tariffs I can't guarantee, but the larger point is that however you save your money, a dollar saved—not spent—is as good, for someone in the 50 percent tax bracket, as *two* of them earned. So while there are limits to this sort of thing (it's fine to shave the cost of the Concorde, but you wouldn't want to fly in coach), you can nonetheless radically improve your personal income statement if you know what corners to cut. Columnist Mike Royko, writing in the Chicago *Sun-Times,* advises that "you can save a considerable sum" on clothing. "The thing to keep in mind," he says, "is that when a suit or shirt or overcoat is wrinkled and soiled—*you don't have to throw it away and buy a new one.* By taking it to a dry cleaning establishment, you can wear it again—*over and over.*"

Just because you are earning zillions in the stock market is no reason to ignore little tips like these. Identical packets of CONTAC cold pills were $2.09 at one pharmacy near me today, $3.95 at another a block away. And for the identical cremation (should CONTAC fail to cure), one of two funeral parlors I called quoted $550, the other, $250.

7. Beware Tax Shelters. You know much more about this than I do and probably have nothing but half interests in terrific little shopping centers bought with positive cash flows and anchored by K-Marts. Since acquiring these properties you have seen occupancy increase and rents skyrocket as the result of some minor landscaping you and your partners decided to do. The bull-semen tax shelters and lithographic-plate tax shelters you would not touch. You *know* about the Clinton Sand geological formation in Ohio, and how even children digging in their sand-boxes out there hit modest but promising strata of hydrocarbons whose porosity becomes unexpectedly problematical twelve minutes after your check has cleared and the limited partnership papers have been filed with the county clerk.

I, on the other hand, am a limited partner in no fewer than seventeen commercially producing oil wells—contracted for when oil was still just $12 a barrel, no less—the income from which, despite more than a doubling in the price of oil, has never quite covered the interest on the loans incurred to drill them.

I am in other more speculative oil deals as well, one of which hit sensationally—truly, it did—until, according to my friend with the joint degrees from Harvard Business School and Harvard Law School who got me to invest, someone dropped a wrench down the well. You or I might have sighed deeply and then either fished out the wrench or, at worst, drilled another hole a few feet to the left; but, strangely, that was the last we limiteds ever heard about either the wrench or the well.

And I am in research-and-development deals and cable TV deals and real estate deals.

I can't honestly say all of these deals have turned out badly, but many of them have, or appear to be waiting their turn in line for the wrench. They remind me of a marvelous line I heard on a radio commercial for something totally unrelated, but which nevertheless applies.

"Other people make empty promises," went the tag line. "We put *ours* in writing."

It's well known (but easily forgotten as the tax year draws to a close) that the first and most crucial test of any "tax deal" is its *economic* merit. Would this deal make sense if there were no tax benefits at all? Is there a profit to be made here *sans* tax advantages? Because if not, as has been shown time and again, it is awfully hard to come out ahead by losing money.

Perhaps one of the reasons real estate has made such good sense as a tax-advantaged investment is that you can see what you're getting, you can understand it (what do we really know about geology or monoclonal antibodies?), you can, in some measure, control it.

8. If It Looks Too Good to Be True, You Haven't Read the Prospectus Carefully Enough. If you've read it at all.

Not that reading a prospectus will help you much to judge whether an investment will fly, unless you happen to be an expert in the business under study, which is why it's wise to fall back on the variant, "If it looks too good to be true, it probably is." Or, "If it *is* so good, why are they offering it to me?" Dentists, particularly, take note.

9. Site Your Tax Havens with Care. It was at a seminar on how to set up offshore captive credit-life-insurance subsidiaries —and you thought my life was dull!—that I learned the drawbacks of two such havens, Minerva and Svalbard. Minerva, we were told, is an island in the South Pacific that offers a totally tax-free environment, but whose inhabitants must sit in their canoes twice a day while their homeland sinks beneath the tide. Svalbard, on the other hand, is an entirely solid little island with a lenient tax code, but cold. A Norwegian protectorate, it is dark from October to March and accessible only by boat.

Twice a month.

In the summer.

10. Buy and Deploy a Video Game. Who says you have to be a mobster to own coin-operated games? Warren Buffett, surely one of the world's dozen most successful investors (chapter 11), got his start deploying pinball machines in barber shops. The problem with pinball machines is that they require a fair amount of service. But not Pac-Man—almost no moving parts. Forget Activision; the Pac-Man you want goes for $2,600 new, no strings attached. Write it off as business equipment and the cost to you, after taxes, is $1,300 or less. Then when your children's friends come over to play—and they will—just watch the quarters pour in. Or make a deal with the local gym teacher to put it in the locker room.

No, that's all wrong. The trick is to locate the thing as far from young people as possible, because young people are able to take one quarter and play for hours at a time. Older folks like ourselves are good for maybe three minutes a shot—$5 an hour. A well-placed machine can easily take in $2,500 a year.

You think I'm wasting your time with penny-ante stuff? You'd rather be in boxcars? Barges? We're talking 100 percent cash-on-cash here. We're talking miniarcades. Multiple minis! Just have your secretary stop off at each on the way to work in the morning, and then at the bank.

Chortle all you want, but before you know it these things are going to be in the parlors of every rest home in the country.

Start your own business. Unless you're young enough to be a rock star or a sports star or a film star, or scuzzy enough to deal drugs, it's your best bet to get rich.

11. "Metromedia Can't Go Down." The importance of this statement was brought home to me after, having shorted Metromedia at 212, it climbed steadily to $560 a share.

In fact, of course (see 5, above), Metromedia *can* go down. A full 65 points one Monday alone. I was *right* to short Metromedia; I just shorted it 348 points too early.

12. Never Underestimate the Power of Compound Interest. The significance of *this* statement is so portentous, so immense, I invite you to freshen your drink before proceeding.

3

COMPOUND INTEREST
Getting Rich Slowly

If you could be any financial concept in the world, which one would you be? Inflation? Hedging? Disintermediation? (Sorry; "rich" is an adjective, not a concept. You've got to pick a concept.) If you were smart, you'd pick compound interest. It never fails to dazzle.

Recently, for example, I bought $200,000 worth of zero-coupon municipal bonds. Zero coupon means they pay no interest. Municipal means I pay no taxes. (Why taxes should be a consideration at all when no interest is paid I shall explain in a minute.) All these bonds offer is the promise that on January 1, 2014, they will be redeemed at full face value: $1,000. I bought 200 such little promises.

Now, even a fine-arts major knows that $1,000 well into the next century is worth something less than $1,000 in cash today. (A bird in the hand, and all that.) But how much less?

I called my broker, a man of surpassing charm and experience, who does things the old-fashioned way. "Buy me two hundred of these New Hampshire zeros of 2014," I said. I love to talk like that.

"At what price?" he asked, quill pen at the ready.

"They're quoted two and five-eighths," I told him.

"What do you mean?" he asked.

"I mean they're quoted two and five-eighths," I explained.

"What do you *mean?*" he asked.

When a bond is quoted at par (100), that means it's selling for 100 cents on the dollar—its full $1,000 face value. When it's quoted at 55, that means it is selling for 55 cents on the dollar. Eventually, it will be redeemed at full face value—$1,000—but right now, if you tried to get rid of it, $550 is all you would get. And when a bond is quoted at two and five-eighths, that means it is selling for two and five-eighths cents on the dollar, or $26.25 a bond. Not a lot of money.

"I mean," I said, "that each bond costs twenty-six dollars and twenty-five cents."

"That can't be right," said my broker. "It must be two sixty-two fifty." The old decimal-point trick. Not $26.25—$262.50.

"Hunh-unh," I explained again, "twenty-six twenty-five."

"You mean," he said, "that for every twenty-six dollars you pay now, you get a thousand dollars in thirty-one years?"

"Now you've got it."

"Wait," he said. "That can't be right."

But it is. And I bought them—$200,000 worth for $5,300. It is the so-called magic of compound interest. It astonished us as children (*Ripley's Believe It or Not!*); it astonishes us today.

I called to tell a young investment-banker friend about these bonds. He holds two Harvard degrees and earned a bonus last year of $73,000. Money is his business. I asked how much he thought it would take to build up $200,000 in after-tax money by 2014.

"You want me to figure it out for you or just guess?" he said.

"Just guess," I said.

"Three thousand a year?"

"No, fifty-three hundred once."

"That can't be right," he said, reaching for his calculator. "What rate of return is that?"

"Twelve percent a year, compounded."

"It is!" he said, a moment later, marveling at the cherry cough syrup display of his pocket calculator.

It was Homer who said that $1,000 invested at a mere 8 percent for 400 years would grow to $23 quadrillion—$5 million for every human on earth. (And you can't see any reason to save?) But, he said, the first 100 years are the hardest. (This was the late Sidney Homer, not Homer Homer—author of the classic *A History of Interest Rates*.)

What invariably happens is that long before the first 100 years are up, someone with access to the cache loses patience. The money burns a hole in his pocket. Or through his nose.

Doubtless that would have been true of the Corrêa fortune, too, had Domingos Faustino Corrêa not cut everyone out of his will for 100 years. That was in 1873, in Brazil. You could have gotten very tired waiting, but if you can establish that you are one of that misanthrope's 4,000-odd legitimate heirs, you may now have some money coming to you. Since 1873, Corrêa's estate has grown, by some estimates, to $12 billion.

Benjamin Franklin had much the same idea, only with higher purpose. Inventive to the end, he left £1,000 each to Boston and Philadelphia. The cities were to lend the money, at interest, to worthy apprentices. Then, after a century, they were to employ part of the fortune Franklin envisioned to construct some public work, while continuing to invest the rest.

One hundred ninety-two years later, when last I checked, Boston's fund exceeded $3 million, even after having been drained to build Franklin Union, and was being lent at interest to medical school students. Philadelphia's fund was smaller, but it, too, had been put to good use. All this from an initial stake of £2,000!

And then there was the king who held a chess tournament among the peasants—I may have this story a little wrong, but the point holds—and asked the winner what he wanted as his prize. The peasant, in apparent humility, asked only that a single kernel of wheat be placed for him on the first square of his chessboard, two kernels on the second, four on the third—and so forth. The king fell for it and had to import grain from Argentina for the next 700 years. Eighteen and a half million trillion kernels, or enough, if each kernel is a quarter-inch long (which it may not be; I've never seen wheat in its pre-English-muffin form), to stretch to the sun and back 391,320 times.

That was nothing more than one kernel's compounding at 100 percent per square for 64 squares. It is vaguely akin to the situation with our national debt.

Just as the peasant could fool the king, so are we peasants fooled now and again. For decades, for example, one of the most basic deceptions in the sale of life insurance has been what is called the net-cost comparison.

Without sitting you down at the kitchen table and walking you through the whole thing (it being difficult to sit and walk simultaneously), suffice it to say that whole-life insurance, seemingly expensive, could be shown by the insurance professional to cost *nothing*. For after twenty or thirty years, your accumulated cash value and dividends could exceed all the premiums you had paid in!

The only thing this comparison ignores is the time value of money—the fact that all those premiums, had they been accruing interest on *your* behalf, might have been worth far more than the amount with which the life insurance company was willing to credit you.

"Do you realize," I have been asked angrily by life insurance salesmen, "that we have policies now that can be paid up after just eight or nine years?" They ask it as if the companies were doing an incredible, unappreciated, magnanimous thing, when, of course, the *reason* no additional premiums are due after the first eight or nine years is simply that the excess charged in those years is enough, when compounded at today's extraordinary interest rates, to fund the policy forever after. There is no magic here, merely the workings of compound interest.

It is remarkable how many people, while they certainly know such terms as interest and return on investment, fail fully to understand them.

Say you borrowed $1,000 from a friend and paid it back at the rate of $100 a month for a year. What rate of interest would that be?

A lot of bright people will answer 20 percent. After all, you borrowed $1,000 and paid back $1,200, so what else could it be? *Forty* percent?

No. More.

If you'd had use of the full $1,000 for a year, then $200 would, indeed, have constituted 20 percent interest. But you had full use of it for only the first month, at the end of which you began paying it back. By the end of the tenth month, far from having use of $1,000, you no longer had use of *any* of the money. So you were paying $200 in the last two months of the year for the right to have used an average of $550 for each of the first ten. That comes to a bit more than a 41.25 percent effective rate of interest. (Trust me.)

Because this sort of thing is complicated, there are truth-in-lending laws requiring creditors to show, in bold type, what they're really charging for money. (Well, they show nominal rates, not effective rates, but it's close enough.) Unfortunately, no similar disclosure law applies to life insurance.

Or tuna fish.

There's this national magazine, you see, which shall remain nameless, that is published by Time, Inc., and that specializes in matters of personal finance. It ran a story two or three years ago, "Bargainmania," about some very strange people— among them, a man who bought 25 years' worth of laundry detergent because it was on sale and a woman who spent the better part of a day and drove 25 miles to buy 18 frozen chickens at 56 cents a pound. The next day, they went on sale at her local market for 53 cents.

One of the people ridiculed in that story was a young and handsome financial writer who shall, in fairness, also remain nameless, but who had bought a case of tuna fish years earlier at his neighborhood supermarket for 59 cents a can. "Yet for all his trouble," the story scoffed (what trouble?), the annual tax-free return on his "investment" will turn out to be only "about eight percent once the tuna is all consumed nearly two years hence."

A letter to the editor, shrill but not hysterical, was dispatched to point out that the magazine had miscalculated. The tax-free rate of return worked out to about *16* percent a year, compounded, not 8.

The point was not so much that the case of tuna fish had turned out to be a reasonable thing to buy—which in its own trivial way it had—but that compound interest and rate-of-return calculations were the sort of thing that a national monthly magazine specializing in personal finance should be able to perform.

In response to the letter came a note from a high-ranking editor at the magazine, saying he wasn't sure they "should be eating crow" just yet and enclosing a "documented analysis" explaining how the 8 percent figure had been arrived at (it had been arrived at wrong)—as though all this were open to opinion rather than a simple matter of mathematics or, simpler still, of punching the appropriate buttons on a pocket calculator. *

---

* For those who have calculators and care:

The magazine assumed that 144 cans of tuna fish had been purchased at 59 cents each (the "investment") and that they were consumed ("sold") at the rate of 25 a year for 5.75 years—at 79 cents the first year, 89 cents the second, 99 cents the third, $1.09 the fourth and (because of an impending tuna glut) 89 cents thereafter.

Some calculators allow you to plug in these numbers, press a button and obtain your result. Or you can look at it this way: The first 25 cans of tuna, eaten over the course of the first year, were "sold" for 79 cents each. If they had all been eaten the last day of the year, that would have been a 20-cent

It was one thing for an error to slip into the story—these things happen. But once the error had been flagged?

If compound interest rate calculations knit your brow, therefore, fret not. You're in distinguished company.

All you really need to know—or a good start, anyway—is the rule of 72. It says: To determine approximately how fast an investment will double, divide the interest rate into 72.

Seventy-two divided by three is twenty-four; money invested at 3 percent, compounded, doubles in just under twenty-four years.

Seventy-two divided by 12 is six; money invested at 12 percent, compounded, doubles in six years. Why does this work? *No one knows.* It works because it's a *rule.* *

Because money invested at 12 percent, compounded, does, indeed, double every six years, in thirty-one-and-a-half years (the time remaining on my 200 New Hampshire zero-coupon bonds), each of my little $26.25 investments will double five times and then grow for another year and a half. At that point, I will be sixty-six (not a pretty thought); the New Hampshire State Housing Authority may or may not be solvent; and a box of Jujyfruits may cost $48.

Wherein lie the two principal risks of these, or any other, long-term bonds: insolvency (what good is a $1,000 promise if it's broken?) and inflation (Jujyfruits have already moved up from a dime a box to half a dollar). If inflation should compound

---

"profit" on each 59-cent purchase, or about 34 percent for the year. But because they were consumed steadily over the course of the year, one every two weeks or so, the *average* can in that first year's batch was held just half a year. The rate of return was, thus, twice as good—about 68 percent. On the next batch of 25 cans, bought for 59 cents and sold over the course of the second year for 89 cents, the profit per can was 30 cents, and the average holding time of the cans was a year and a half. To earn 30 cents on 59 cents in a year and a half is to earn 31.5 percent compounded annually. Only on the last few cans would the compounded annual rate of return have been eight percent.

* Actually, it has something to do with the natural logarithm of 2, but I skipped that class.

as fast as my bonds, then $200,000 in 2014 will buy precisely what $5,300 buys today.

But should inflation and interest rates return to "normal" levels any time soon—4 percent having been a perfectly respectable return on municipal bonds throughout much of this century, and 6 percent having been the rate as recently as 1978 —then I will be sitting pretty indeed, watching my bonds compound tax-free at 12 percent. (There is one teensy-weensy catch here, to which I will return.)

Others will have locked in high yields on interest-bearing thirty-year bonds, but they will not be sitting so pretty. Most long-term bonds issued today include "call" provisions. Today's municipals are typically callable after ten years. At that point, they can be paid off. You may be locked into the Reno Desalinization Project for forty years, but the Reno Desalinization Project is locked into you for only ten. Thus, just as *you* may be planning to refinance your high-interest mortgage when interest rates drop, so are most states and cities hoping to refinance *their* high-interest debt.

Most zero-coupon bonds can't be called. What good would it do? Calling a bond ordinarily means buying it back at par or a little above. So—go ahead! Buy back my little $26.25 investments at $1,000 each! That is something even the feeblest of state controllers is not likely to propose.

In the event that interest rates do fall, there is a second enormous advantage to zero-coupon bonds. Not only am I guaranteed my 12 percent until 2014—it is 12 percent *compounded.* Purchasers of ordinary long-term bonds may continue to get high interest—but what will they earn in interest *on that?* A bond that pays 12 percent but from which the interest can be reinvested at only, say, 6 percent, will grow not to $1,000 from $26.25 by the year 2014 but to a paltry $305.

So much for the advantages of zero-coupon bonds. Bear in mind the following:

1. As with any long-term bonds, the issuer could go broke

(except that in the case of the most common zeroes, the so-called CATS and TIGRs and the like, the issuer is, in effect, the U.S. Treasury, and there's not much to worry about).

2. Likewise, if interest rates rise, the value of the zero-coupon bond will fall. Eventually, it will rise to its full $1,000 face value, but eventually is a long way off.

3. The Internal Revenue Service was not born yesterday. Even though zero-coupon bonds pay no interest, you are taxed as if they did. If the bond is geared to grow by 12 percent a year to maturity, then you pay tax each year as if you'd received 12 percent interest. (The exception: municipal zeros, which, like any other municipal bonds, are federal income-tax-free.)

Obviously, this makes taxable zero-coupon bonds a crummy investment, except for tax-sheltered funds, such as IRAs and Keogh plans. (There they are excellent. Call your broker for details.)

4. Although you can sell zero-coupon bonds, like any other long-term bond, any time you want, the market in most of these issues will be thin. Thin, inactive markets mean big spreads for the market makers.

5. The advantages of zero-coupon bonds and their handiness with respect to IRAs and Keoghs will be reflected in their price. The more popular they become, the less attractive they will be. My New Hampshire State Housing Authority zeros, purchased at $26.25, will yield 12 percent, compounded, to maturity. By January 1985, other things being equal, they should have risen to about $38 on their long 12 percent compounded climb to $1,000. Should they have been bid up to, say, $65 instead, there would be substantially less incentive to buy them, for at that price they would be yielding only 9.9 percent to maturity. *

* How do I know this so fast? I press 65 on my Texas Instruments MBA calculator and then the button marked PV (present value—what I'm paying today). Then I press 1,000 and the FV button (future value—what I'll get, God willing, tommorrow). Then I press 29 and the N button (the number of years until tomorrow). Then I press CPT (compute) percent I (interest rate). I wait exactly two seconds. During this time (as I understand it), a message is

6. In the case of this particular New Hampshire State Housing Authority bond issue there is the aforementioned teensy-weensy little catch. *Most* zero-coupon bonds can't be called. As I've said, what good would it do? But these and some other zero-coupon municipals are callable at the issuer's discretion— *not* at their ultimate $1,000 face value, but in accordance with an "accretion schedule" that starts at a pittance, like your bond, and rises each year at 12 percent.

So if long-term interest rates drop dramatically, say goodbye to your New Hampshire zeros. They will be called back in by the Housing Authority. Just one more example of the Eighth Law of Finance: IF IT LOOKS TOO GOOD TO BE TRUE, YOU HAVEN'T READ THE PROSPECTUS.

I could tell you about *sub*zero coupon bonds, where you pay *them* interest; but these are not yet off the drawing board (or on it, so far as I know). I could tell you about tontines, in which not only your money but the money of all your grade school classmates compounds magnificently on your behalf, should you be the last one left alive to claim it; but these have fallen out of fashion.

Available and in fashion are the aforementioned IRAs and Keogh plans. IRAs provide a discipline to save (the discipline comes in the extra taxes you pay if you don't save), and they also allow money, once under the IRA umbrella, to compound free of taxes.

But is there really any reason for a man or woman in his or her twenties, say, and maybe not even in so high a tax bracket, to bother with one of these things?

---

bounced off a satellite and down to Texas Instruments, where a fellow in a green eyeshade with a cactus on his desk whips out paper and pencil, does the calculation and shoots it back up to New York before the Japanese even know that there has been a little bit of business to bid on. This is the same fellow who used to do the customized research reports for the owners of the *Encyclopaedia Britannica* that always used to arrive a week or two after your term paper was due. He's gotten much faster.

Far be it from me to counsel anything so dull. I have most of my own fortune tied up in Japanese antiques (four-year-old video-tape recorders). But did you know that $2,000 compounded at 8 percent (after taxes) grows to $43,449 in forty years—*but to $377,767* at 14 percent sheltered from taxes in an IRA? Or that putting away $2,000 a year at 12 percent, beginning at the age of thirty-five, builds to $482,665 by sixty-five— *but to $1,534,183* if you start ten years earlier?

However little $377,767 will buy in forty years, it will buy more than $43,449. However paltry $1,534,183, it will be less paltry than $482,665.

Two final notes:

(1) The national magazine eventually saw the light.

(2) The 1984 tax bill closed a gaping loophole with regard to zero-coupon municipals—but not entirely. It used to be—outrageously—that if you bought a $1,000 zero-coupon municipal bond 30 years from maturity for $40 and sold it two years later for $50, you'd report a whopping *loss*. You'd say, "Well, I bought it for $40, which means it'll have to appreciate $32 a year to reach $1,000 in 30 years." In fact, that's totally wrong. It rises just a little in the early years and, with compounding, by leaps and bounds near the end. But the law ignored this. "So [you'd say], by the time I sold it for $50, it should really have grown to $104—the $40 I paid plus $32 for each year I held it. The difference between the $104 it should have been and the $50 I got is my loss." Both you and the IRS knew this was silly, but both you and the IRS knew this was the law. You got a profit but reported a loss. Amazingly, the 1984 tax bill left this loophole open for purchasers of municipal zeroes *issued before September 3, 1982*. Caveat: the price of such rarities will doubtless rise to reflect their magic quality; check with your accountant before plunging in in any significant way.

4

INSIDE INFORMATION
Getting Rich Quick

There are two kinds of information on Wall Street: the information that is flashed over the wire services the instant it's available, and the information that circulates beforehand. Inside information.

The first thing to know about inside information is that using it is illegal. You could go to jail for five years. The second thing to know is that no one ever has, although lesser penalties are meted out from time to time.

(There is a third kind of information with which Wall Street is awash—unimportant information; and a fourth kind—misinformation; but here our concern is with important, accurate information of the kind that will really move a stock. Like the news that Warner Communications would report dismal earnings for the fourth quarter of 1982. Warner stock dropped from 52 to 35 in one day. Who could have anticipated such news? Surely not the eight executives of Warner's Atari division who had sold thousands of shares in the weeks preceding.)

In the previous chapter it was noted how, through the power of compounding, even a small sum, given time, could grow bountifully large. But who has time? The way to make a killing fast is with inside information. I do not recommend this. It is illegal; it is unfair; it frequently backfires.

It is hard to resist.

Had you known in advance, for example, that Kuwait's national oil company would acquire Santa Fe International in the fall of 1981, you need only have ponied up $37.50 for an option on 100 Santa Fe shares to realize $1,925 a week later. Buy 100 such options and . . . well, you can figure it out.

One Santa Fe executive allegedly privy to the deal called his broker in Dallas all the way from China to get in on the action.

A wealthy Kuwaiti called Merrill Lynch (open there from nine A.M. to midnight) and bought options on 50,000 shares. Days later, Kuwait Petroleum Corporation made its offer and Faisal al-Massoud al-Fuhaid was richer by $840,000—a seventeenfold profit in two weeks. Confronted with charges that he had acted on inside information, al-Fuhaid was contemptuous. "If I had known of [the deal in advance]," he huffed, "I would have bought much more than just $1,000,000 worth of shares!"

(An odd defense, in that it acknowledges al-Fuhaid's readiness to do the very thing he was accused of, only bigger. The matter is being litigated.)

But who's to argue? It is not always the easiest thing to know —for certain—whether a fellow's been tipped off to "material, nonpublic information," as it's called, or whether he's just been lucky. People do occasionally score big in the market legitimately. Shortly before Kuwait Petroleum made its bid for Santa Fe, one clever fellow with no apparent connection to either company bought 600 options—he just called his discount broker and placed the order—turning a few thousand dollars into $1,000,000 in a matter of days. Did he know something? He got the idea, he told the Securities and Exchange Commission, from reading *Forbes*. The SEC was satisfied.

And it's true: Inside information *is* just the stuff you find in magazines or the newspaper. Next week's newspaper. If it's today's newspaper, you're too late.

I flew to Australia a few years ago and told my broker I was going. My broker makes much more money than I do (who wants a poor broker?), but he is desk-bound. Others blow $30 on a two-hour lunch; he makes $300 eating a tuna-salad sandwich and a pickle at his desk. One of the secrets of his success has been, simply, availability. He's there when you need him (and frequently on the phone to you when you don't). The only days he gets to travel are the days the market is closed, and, as you can't tour too many European capitals on a long weekend, the one thing I can do to get back at him for making so much more money than I do is to send him postcards and phone him collect from exotic places. He pretends not to care. "There are lots of terrific things to see and do right here in New York!" he tells me, as I'm jetting off to Akron or Dubuque.

The point of all this is that when I jetted off to Sydney and told him the time difference (Australia is a day ahead of New York), he became suddenly quiet. Even a bit respectful, I thought. "Hello?" I said. He said nothing, but I could hear him thinking.

"It's tomorrow in Australia?" he finally said. "You mean, if it's Monday afternoon here, it's Tuesday morning in Australia?" The human voice is an infinitely expressive thing; it was no mystery what he had in mind.

"Oh, come on—don't be ridiculous," I said.

But imagine being able to know what the market was going to do a day in advance. Imagine getting a day's jump on the rest of the world. Genentech gonna drop five points tomorrow? Think I'll short some today. American Express gonna announce a bid for Federal Express tomorrow? Think I'll buy a call on Federal Express.

It's not very sportsmanlike, like memorizing the backs of the blanks in Scrabble (or, if you pull the tiles out of a bag, learning to read them with your fingertips); but if you don't mind cheating, it works.

If caught, you will ordinarily be forced by the SEC to do two things (and only two things). You will be forced to "disgorge" your profit, and you will be forced to sign a consent decree agreeing not to violate securities laws in the future. The publicity attendant on all this may also wreck your career (it could be some time before David J. Winans, the *Wall Street Journal* reporter who repeatedly leaked word of his "Heard on the Street" columns, gets another job with a major national newspaper)—but it may not. It depends on your profession and the sensibilities of the crowd you run with. Late in 1981, the SEC charged former Secretary of the Air Force Thomas C. Reed with turning $3,125 into $427,000—in forty-eight hours—on a tip from his dad, a director of AMAX. Reed disgorged his profit (stick your finger down your throat when you say that) and signed the consent decree amid a good deal of national publicity; he was then appointed to the White House National Security Council staff as a special assistant to President Reagan.

The SEC would prefer stiffer civil penalties and is close to winning them from Congress. For if all you can lose by breaking the law is what you've gained—hey, give it back—where's the risk in trying? Yes, the Justice Department can institute a criminal action subjecting you to a maximum $10,000 fine and five years in jail for each count of insider trading; but few cases have been brought and almost no one has been incarcerated. That is true in part because insider trading is hard to prove, and in part because it pales before some of the other wrongdoing an overworked Justice Department is trying to fight, and so receives low priority. It is perceived by many as a victimless crime. Semantha Seller, who knows nothing, decides to sell her stock. For whatever reason. No one has tricked her into it. Bubba Buyer buys it. The next day, a tender offer is announced and the stock doubles. If Buyer had not known of the deal—as he might well not have—then Seller is merely the victim of bad luck. If, on the other hand, Buyer was acting on inside information, then—though the consequences to Seller are identical—Seller is the victim of a crime. Either way, it was her desire to sell the stock; either way, she got the going price for it—so how has she been harmed?

Actually, you could argue that Seller got an even better price than she would have if insiders hadn't been in the market bidding up the price of the stock. (On the other hand, you could argue that had they not bid it up, she would not have been tempted to sell.) But if insider trading causes relatively little harm to individual victims, it is harmful in a more fundamental way. For if investors perceive that the game is rigged and that they don't have a fair chance, they may reasonably decide not to play. To the extent that they withdraw from the equity markets, everyone suffers. Prosperity depends on investment. Broad, healthy capital markets are one of America's principal assets.

So even in an administration not noted for harassing the rich, it is not surprising, when you think about it, that the war on insider trading is going strong. The abuse, like tax fraud, will never be eradicated, but the SEC is trying to "raise the level of risk." More insider-trading actions have been filed since 1980 —upwards of 80—than in the preceding four decades. And there's been progress against one huge loophole: the assured anonymity of trading through Swiss banks. It's not assured anymore.

Still, questions of law and philosophy remain. Just how important must information be to be "material"? Just who is an insider?

Were the good people of Des Moines insiders back in the winter of 1978, when they began to notice planeloads of merger and acquisition specialists arriving at the Equitable of Iowa Companies from the prestigious law offices of Cravath, Swaine & Moore in New York? The good people of Des Moines know an opportunity when it smacks 'em in the face. They began buying stock in the Equitable. A stock that had budged barely half a point all winter suddenly found itself up 25 percent in three days. Trading in the stock was halted.

On Friday, it was announced that, sure enough, the folks from Cravath had been in town to do an acquisition. Only Equitable was to be the acquisitor, not the acquisitee. The good folks of Des Moines should have been buying stock in the Provident Life Insurance Company of Bismarck, North Dakota. (The good folks of Bismarck, North Dakota, were apparently doing just that. Someone was. Its stock, too, ran up sharply before the news hit.) On Monday, the Equitable reopened for trading at $20 a share, down $6. "A sure way to lose money in the take-over game," commented *Barron's* Alan Abelson "is to confuse the taker with the takee."

A young theatrical agent called me with inside information about a stock whose name he'd forgotten. A stockbroker friend had told him the company was about to be taken over. Should he buy options on the stock, as the broker had urged? "Oh, come on," I said. "If it were really being taken over, do you think you would know about it?" Well, the broker was a very close friend of his, and he had a source deep inside the company. "In that case," I said, "you should buy an option. You will almost surely lose your $300, but you're obviously itching to do this. And in the extraordinary event that the information proves accurate and you haven't hopped on board, you will never forgive either one of us." He was positively giddy at the prospect of a quick killing. The fact that it might be illegal seemed, if anything, to make the whole deal more intriguing.

"Do you remember anything about the company?" I asked. "Anything at all?"

"I remember it's at 28."

"Pittston!" I snorted. ("Piss on you, too," he said.) I knew it was Pittston for three reasons. First, Pittston was around 28 (it's 11 as I write this). Second, it was one of the couple of hundred stocks (now there are 355) on which options were traded. Third, everybody in the world had heard the rumor that Pittston, a coal-mining, armored-truck outfit mired in adversity, was going to be acquired at some sensational price, and the rumor had apparently, at last, reached my friend the theatrical agent. He bought the option; he lost his money.

Those of us who have an interest in the stock market are deluged with what is purported to be inside information. A good rule of thumb in such situations is to ignore it. Not always having the maturity to follow such good rules, I bought Pittston options, too. The difference is, my naïve friend actually thought he might make some big money. I knew I would lose mine.

Were this idiot and I insiders? Would we have been had someone actually acquired Pittston? (Someone eventually will. The trick is to have it happen in your lifetime and, more to the point, before your options expire.)

I know that strings of unanswered questions make trying reading—reminding us, as they do, of exams—but 'try to get into the spirit of the thing and answer these:

If you somehow know that market vaudevillian Joe Granville is going to send out a buy signal tomorrow, is it unfair to buy today? If you know that analyst Marty Zweig, who's been on a hot streak, is going to recommend Standard Microsystems to his 19,000 subscribers tomorrow, is it unfair to buy today? What if you know that the *Wall Street Journal* is going to be coming out with a highly favorable story on Chi-Chi's, a Mexican-restaurant chain (reporting, among other things, that Chi-Chi's hot sauce retards hair loss)? What if you *wrote* the story? What if you merely proofread it? What if you found an advance proof on the subway? What if you heard about that draft from your mother-in-law? ("Sidney, our prayers have been answered. Sidney, do you hear what I'm saying to you?") What if the draft you wrote or proofread or picked up on the subway was about Chi-Chi's stock but was devastatingly negative— could you short the stock? Could you at least sell the fifty shares you happened to own? What if you had been planning to sell those shares anyway—would you now have an obligation to hold on to them and watch them fall?

I could go on. There's a world of subtlety here I've barely scratched. Stanley Sporkin, the SEC's former chief of enforcement, tried to cut through it. According to Sporkin, if someone —anyone—trades on the basis of important information that's not yet publicly available, he or she has violated the law. Say you are landing at an airport, Sporkin told an audience once, and from the air, you see a company's principal plant burning. Seconds later, on the ground, you race to a pay phone to short the stock. Is that good luck and quick thinking? No, said Sporkin, it's a crime.

And if, instead of shorting the stock, you merely bought stock in the company's chief competitor? Well, Sporkin said, if news of the fire could be expected to have a material impact on that stock, it would be a crime as well.

Obviously, no one at the SEC would treat such a case—if he treated it at all—in the same way he'd treat the case of an investment banker who repeatedly traded on privileged information. But the SEC has gone after a health club employee who found out from Mrs. Johnny Carson that her husband might be cutting a deal with National Kinney to promote a Las Vegas hotel. (He ultimately didn't, but news of the deal sent the stock up.) And it has gone after the father of a stockbroker who was sleeping with a paralegal who was, innocently, letting things slip about her firm's clients.

Certainly, Nathan Rothschild would have died in jail had King George III had an SEC and had Messrs. Shad and Fedders (current chairman and chief of enforcement) been around to run it. Rothschild, as is well known, had pigeons. He was forever getting little tidbits of information—such as the British defeat of Napoleon at Waterloo—and using them to advantage. Waterloo, to take that example, was not the sort of news that, when it became known, would be buried on page three. But rather than merely buying quietly and reaping a fat profit, Rothschild, by some accounts, sold quietly. His quiet selling was soon picked up by those who watched his every move (they all knew he had pigeons), and everyone sold in a panic. Rothschild then moved in and bought in much greater volume and at much lower prices than he otherwise could have (really quietly this time, which he knew how to do), selling at a huge profit when the news finally reached England.

It's not hard to profit from a situation when you're the only one who knows what's going on.

In 1978, the SEC charged Saul Steinberg (the mogul, not the artist) with having persuaded Beverly Hills businessman James Randall and actor George Hamilton to buy stock in a company called Pulte Home "by informing them that a take-over attempt of Pulte by 'the Rockefellers' was about to occur. The purported take-over attempt was fabricated by Steinberg to increase the market price of Pulte stock, thereby affording him the opportunity to sell [at an inflated price]."

Not only did the SEC go after Steinberg, it went after Randall and Hamilton, charging that they had bought Pulte on inside information (even though it was only fake inside information) and thus they had violated the law.

Steinberg and Randall and Hamilton, reported the SEC, "without admitting or denying the allegations in the Complaint" (no one ever does) "consented to Judgments of Permanent Injunction enjoining them from violating Section 10(b) of the Exchange Act and Rule 10b-5."

In the colorful world of W-2 and 1040EZ, 501c-3 and K-1, 10-K and 13D—10b-5 is right up there. You get in trouble with 10b-5 and you is in big trouble.

Inside information is tricky, tricky stuff. First, you have to be sure you really have it. Then you have to persuade yourself you really don't. And even if you really do have it and know you really do have it and have persuaded yourself you really don't have it (so it's OK to use it), you still have to guess what it means.

Let's say OPEC is going to drop its posted price for a barrel of oil from \$34 to \$29—and only you know about it! Do you sell the oil stocks short? Not necessarily. For some—because they'd been stuck buying oil at the posted price and selling it to the world at the lower spot price—a drop in official oil prices turned out to be good news.

But why deal in hypotheticals?

"Three days ago," says a friend of mine, "a guy calls me up from the Gulf [not the Gulf of Mexico, you understand] and says, 'Sit down.'

" 'OK,' I tell him, 'I'm sitting down.'

"He says, 'Allied is going to bid for 27½ percent of Bendix —let's buy Bendix.' (Not the whole thing; just 10,000 or 20,000 shares.)

"I said no.

"He said, 'Why not? They're going to bid 85.' (Bendix was then 57.)

"I said, 'Don't you see? If they're just going to bid for 27½ percent of the company, the stock will go *down*.' "

Bendix, at 57, had already had quite a run, because Martin Marietta was trying to acquire it. (Martin Marietta was trying to acquire it because it was trying to acquire Martin Marietta. Each was gobbling up the other.) My friend reasoned that Allied's bid was—and would be perceived by the market as—a friendly deal designed to rescue Bendix from being taken over at any price. Otherwise, why would Allied be bidding for just 27½ percent?

Savvy guy, my friend.

"If anything," he said, "you shouldn't buy Bendix—you should short it." The stock, he felt, would probably fall four or five points on the news, as those who'd hoped Bendix would be acquired by Marietta saw their dream foiled and dumped their stock.

"OK," said the man from the Gulf, eager to derive at least some gain from his privileged information and not too particular how, "let's short it, then."

"So," my friend continues, "we shorted a few thousand Bendix"—hey, let's not go overboard—"and it turned out he had 90 percent of the story 100 percent correct." Allied did, indeed, make a bid for Bendix at 85 ("Obviously, he had a source inside Allied," says my friend), but instead of bidding for 27½ percent, they bid for the whole thing. Bendix shares, far from falling four or five points, opened 17 points higher.

Getting it a little wrong can be very painful.

"We had a similar situation with Gulf and Cities Service," my friend adds. "We had information that Mesa was going to be bought out by Cities, so we bought options on Mesa. But Gulf tendered for Cities, and our options, which expired the following week, expired worthless."

In both of these cases, inside information was clearly leaking out and being used illegally. But what is the SEC to do—force the insiders to disgorge their losses? Reimburse them?

It's not an unusual number of larcenous friends that provide me with such a stock of insider-trading anecdotes. It is, rather, that the abuse of inside information is so widespread.

It's widespread because all but the most blatant abuses go unchecked. Say you find out Pittston really is being taken over. You really know. (Well, you're the company's lawyer, let's say, or its vice-president of finance.) Rather than buy stock yourself or even for your brother-in-law, you call someone equally well placed and say, "Charlie, don't say anything—do you recognize my voice?—just write this down: Pittston, Tuesday, at 45. Got it? You owe me one."

Charlie, no fool, buys a bunch of Pittston and a few weeks later makes a huge profit. Sometime in the future, he returns the favor. If his purchase of Pittston is large enough or comes just days or hours before a deal is announced, the SEC may come a-calling—as well it should. But Charlie, who owns dozens of stocks and makes scores of transactions a year, says he bought the stock because he thought steel would be rebounding (Pittston supplies metallurgical coal), or because its chart looked good, or because—anything. It's one thing if Henry Ford's maid, who owns nothing but a $100,000 savings certificate, buys 200 way-out-of-the-money calls on Ford the day before Ford announces resumption of its dividend; quite another if Charlie, who's in and out of a dozen positions a week, happens to get lucky in one of them.

On Thursday, May 13, 1982, 127 puts were purchased on Chase Manhattan Bank stock. (You buy puts if you think a stock is going to go down.) It was a slow-to-average day for Chase puts. On Friday, volume doubled. Two hundred fifty-two puts were purchased. And on Monday, a day before disclosure of the Drysdale Government Securities fiasco that left Chase in deep snit, 975 puts were purchased. Just coincidence probably. The stock plunged and the gleeful put holders used their profits to buy tasteful works of art and repave their driveways.

Just before Sears announced its offer to acquire Dean Witter Reynolds, Dean Witter stock jumped 20 percent. In the month preceding Prudential's offer for Bache, Bache stock moved up 43 percent.

Well, it's tough to keep these things secret!

Seventy-nine percent of corporate-take-over targets examined in one study experienced a trading surge the week before the news hit. In another, *Fortune* chose twenty takeover targets at random and found that stock in all but one had moved up significantly in the month before the deal was announced. To some extent, that might have resulted from last-minute buying in the open market by the acquiring company. But some, if not most, of the extra trading doubtless came from excited tippees.

"It's just another of those stories," a broker friend told me, "but El Paso is supposed to be the next one to go." Because it was just another of those stories (whoever said there were 8 million stories in the naked city was underestimating), I ignored it. A week later, Burlington Northern made its bid for El Paso Natural Gas. I could have been rich!

To thwart widespread abuse of inside information, the SEC has been lobbying Congress for authority to seek disgorgement of *triple* an insider's ill-gotten profits. That should give its civil proceedings real bite. A lot of casual players in this game, and some not so casual, are likely to think a lot harder before placing their bets.

The SEC also hopes for better success in the courts.

Kenneth Rubinstein attended New York University Law School and went to work for Fried, Frank, Harris, Shriver & Jacobson in New York in 1979. He had been there thirty months when he learned the SEC was investigating him on seven counts of insider trading. He resigned from the law firm and subsequently disgorged his profits and signed a consent decree. Although signing the consent decree is neither an admission nor a denial of guilt, it is not the sort of thing that advances a young counselor's career. So in Rubinstein's case, without its ever having gone to court, you might say the SEC was successful.

But Rubinstein's brother Aaron, also an attorney (Kaye, Scholer, Fierman, Hayes & Handler), had also profited from Kenneth's inside information. So the SEC charged him as well. Unlike Kenneth, Aaron fought the charges, admitting that he had bought the stocks on his brother's recommendation, but denying that he had ever known he was receiving privileged information. (As one after another of the stocks he bought zoomed on takeover news, he apparently just figured his brother was one heck of a stock picker.) Federal judge Morris E. Lasker ruled in his favor. "We conclude," he concluded, "that in spite of the substantial—some might call it massive—circumstantial evidence . . . the commission didn't meet the burden of establishing its case." So Aaron got to keep his $311,000 profit and was, when last we checked, still an associate at Kaye, Scholer, Fierman, Hayes & Handler.

There was no question that he had profited from inside information. He was allowed to keep the profit because he might not have known it was inside information.

Equally awkward for the SEC, and better known, was the case of Vincent Chiarella.

Chiarella was a mark-up man in the composing room of Pandick Press, a financial printer. He worked on prospectuses involved with corporate takeovers. It's true they arrived in his hands with the corporate names left blank or disguised (the real names to be supplied the night before the actual printing), but Chiarella was able to deduce from the prospectuses who the takeover targets were. He cleared $30,000 in trading profits over fourteen months. In May 1977, he signed an SEC consent decree, agreed to return the money and was fired. That was the civil side of the action. Then he was indicted on seventeen counts of securities fraud and convicted. When his conviction was upheld on appeal, his case ultimately reached the Supreme Court. The Court ruled, in 1980, that because Chiarella had no fiduciary relationship with the sellers, nor any prior dealings with them of any kind, he had not defrauded them. His conviction was overturned.

Chief Justice Warren Burger was one of the dissenters. "The evidence shows beyond all doubt," he argued, "that Chiarella, working literally in the shadows of the warning signs in the print shop, misappropriated—stole, to put it bluntly—valuable nonpublic information entrusted to him in the utmost confidence. He then exploited his ill-gotten informational advantage by purchasing securities in the market. In my view, such conduct plainly violates . . . Rule 10b-5."

But that was the minority view.

To redress the Chiarella verdict, the SEC wrote a further regulation—as yet untested—requiring anyone with knowledge of an undisclosed tender offer to tell the seller the news before purchasing stock.

If the Chiarella case was the SEC's most noted insider-trading setback, perhaps its most noted success—on the front page for days—was the case against my friend and former business-school sectionmate Adrian Antoniu, his friend Jacques Courtois (another classmate), three confederates and a Long Island dentist. (The dentist was a sort of footnote. He had paid one of the five cash in exchange for information.)

Adrian had arrived here from Romania as a child and—only in America—wound up at Morgan Stanley, and then at Kuhn Loeb, as an investment banker. With the relatively small killing he made trading on inside information (hundreds of thousands, not millions), he lived, on Park Avenue, better than any of us could explain. The first clue came in the summer of 1978, when we began getting phone calls from Venice. Adrian was in the sinking city to marry Francesca Stanfill, daughter of then 20th Century-Fox chairman Dennis Stanfill—no small affair. The cardinal (soon to become Pope John Paul I) was among those who sent congratulations. But even as all this was going on, the SEC was closing in. And Adrian knew it. He was ducking out of the festivities to call his friends back home with a simple, if cryptic, request: "If you get any calls from the SEC, I'd really appreciate it if you'd call my lawyer before saying anything."

The SEC wrapped up its investigation; the marriage was annulled. Adrian was booted out of his job. He agreed to cooperate with the government, pleaded guilty to charges of securities fraud and works now for an international executive-search firm in Milan. After a great deal of legal hoop-de-doo, he was spared a four-month prison term. Even so, the cheerfulness in his voice is gone.

Courtois, meanwhile, son of a prominent Canadian, left Morgan Stanley before he was indicted—left North America, in fact —and married a Radcliffe alum, niece of the former president of Colombia, in Bogotá. For several years, the U.S. failed to get Courtois extradited—he went into flower exporting—but in 1984 he returned to the U.S. for sentencing. Six months in jail and disgorgement of $150,000 of an estimated $400,000 in illegal profits.

There's a certain knowing humor to all this. Most people who trade stocks have at least some idea of the role inside information plays. Some, I think, even exaggerate its importance. (Others would say that's hard to do.) Yet, rather than be incensed by it, most folks merely hope to get in on the action.

R. Neil Blake had no inside information when he began playing the stock market. He got involved, reports *The Seattle Times'* Gary Heberlein, to take his mind off his recent divorce and the suicide of his teenaged daughter. And for about a year, all was well. In exactly the kind of active options trading prudent investment advisers would have begged him not to undertake, Blake had turned $20,000 into $40,000. And on Thursday, October 1, 1981, he was sitting with a pile of Santa Fe options that, unbeknown to him, would within less than an hour lock him into a further $39,000 profit. All he had to do was nothing. Instead, despairing of Santa Fe's ever being able to rise from $24.625, its price then, to better than $30 a share within the next eleven trading days, as it had to for his options to be worth anything, he sold them all. In fact, to pick up an extra $375 (less tax and commission), he sold more than he owned. That was a safe thing to do as long as Santa Fe did, indeed, remain below 30. Instead, as a result of the Kuwaiti acquisition, it opened the following Monday in the mid-40s. Blake was nearly wiped out.

One could argue that he would have been equally devastated had no one profited illegally from the Santa Fe takeover. He would still have sold those options and would still have been walloped when the news broke. In that sense, there's no harm in insider trading.

But "in the final analysis," former SEC commissioner A. A. Sommer has said, "insider trading is wrong, dreadfully and viciously wrong. It undermines our markets, cheapens and tarnishes the integrity of our system and hopefully, if we are vigilant enough, it may increasingly impoverish those who engage in it.''

Some of them, anyway.

5

FANCY FOOTWORK
Getting Rich Smart

It's time to talk with you about great plays. Not stuff like *Night of the Iguana* or *The Frogs,* though I'll grant there's some money in those, too—I'm talking about the kind of play where you dive into the third market and buy 40,000 Kodak, butterfly the July and October options, link the two with a pile of September silvers, hedge with market-index options and interest-rate futures, close out the whole thing an hour later and leave for the helipad $408,000 to the good.

Not because you're greedy; because life's a game. (As a currently popular T-shirt has it: WHOEVER HAS THE MOST THINGS WHEN HE DIES, WINS. There's not much room for subtlety on a T-shirt.)

A lot of people think that if they were just smarter, they could make a ton of money in the market. Wrong! Smart alone won't do it. It's important also to be lucky, to have the right temperament and to have a good-sized stake to begin with. (The rich get richer, in part, because they can afford to take risks and to be patient.) It may also help to put in the hours. Not sitting in a broker's gallery eyeballing the ticker day after day—that won't help. *Digging for something special.*

Among the several methods:

1. What is loosely known as the Benjamin Graham approach, after the late father of fundamental analysis, in which you analyze balance sheet after balance sheet until you find a company selling so blatantly beneath its net-asset value that you need not even sample its products or interview its management to know it's a good bet—a situation much less prevalent today than just a few years ago, which is why this proved so profitable for the folks who made the effort a few years ago.

2. What might be called the arbitrageur's approach, which consists of finding wonderful little lapses of logic in the prices of related securities and exploiting the bejesus out of them.

The first approach—hunting for value and then sitting tight —is widely known. The second—dancing around the edges of the game, looking for clever openings—is less often described. To quote Webster:

> AR'BI TRAGE: Like when you see gold trading at $420 an ounce in London and at $422 in New York and you buy 1 million ounces in London at the time as you sell them in New York and you pocket the $2 million spread. Like, man—it's fantastic.

Not everyone is adept at this sort of thing.

I called a classmate who will earn $500,000 this year as an institutional salesman (not selling institutions, selling *to* them— as contrasted with "retail" salesmen, who sell securities to "the public"). He's smart—and quick. I said, "Listen, Hotshot [not his real name], I need an example of something really brilliant you've done, something that involves a couple of different securities and some fancy footwork or a wrinkle. Give me an example of some great idea you've had and you'll be famous."

He immediately grasped the concept, then fell silent. "I know what you mean," he finally said, "but I can't think of anything."

"Oh, come on—just one idea!"

More silence.

"I can just see what you're going to write," he chortled. " 'Been in the business fifteen years, never had an idea.' "

THE WARNER PLAY:
BUY THE STOCK, SHORT THE WARRANTS

I start with this one because it's one of two I've thought of myself. (Been in the business fifteen years, had two ideas.) It has to do with the stock of Warner Communications.

Warner hit an all-time high of 63 in 1982. It was not of much interest at that price, at least to me, because I've always been a sucker for the notion of "buying low"—a discipline that of necessity precludes buying stocks at or near their all-time highs.

Not long afterward, Warner announced that its Atari division was in the tank and the stock dropped to 28¼.

In toying with the notion of buying some—at that price, it looked interesting—I remembered Warner warrants. A warrant gives you the right to buy stock at some specified price (55 in this case) for a given length of time (through April 30, 1986, in this case). Warrants are also called rights, because that's all they are: the right to buy stock at a certain price. They could be called options, too, for they operate in much the same way; only warrants are issued by the underlying company itself, while options are issued by bookies* in Chicago, New York, Philadelphia and San Francisco. Also, options run for a maximum of nine months, while warrants generally do not expire for several years.

The Warner warrant trades on the American Stock Exchange. I figured if it were cheap enough, it might be a better

* So to speak.

way to bet on Warner's future than simply to buy the stock. But what's cheap enough? What is the right to buy a stock at 55—when it's 28—worth? Clearly, that depends on how long the warrant has to run (the longer, the better) and how likely the stock is to shoot up in price.

My guess was that the warrant would be selling around 5. For $500, that is, you could purchase the right to buy 100 shares of Warner stock at $55 each through April 1986. For $5,000, you could control *1,000* shares. Buying 1,000 shares outright, by contrast, would have cost $28,250.

I'm not saying I would have bought the warrants at 5, but that's about what I figured they were worth.

I looked in the paper (WrnC wt) and was astonished to find them, in fact, at 11¼. People were actually plunking down $11.25 to control shares of Warner stock that they could have *owned* for $28.25 in the wild hope that sometime this side of April 30, 1986, Warner would climb from 28¼ to well past 55. Which just goes to show there's no telling what folks will pay for little pieces of paper and a dream.

But if it's hard to know what a warrant like this is worth with three years left to run, here's almost exactly what it will be worth on the morning of expiration:

If Warner stock is:	The right to buy it at $55 will be worth:
$ 55 or below	$ 0
65	10
75	20
100	45

Only if the stock were above $66 a share would the right to buy it at $55 be worth more than $11 at expiration.

The stock, at 28¼, seemed perhaps undervalued. The warrant, at 11¼, seemed ridiculously *over*valued. So here was the play: *Buy the stock and short the warrants.* (Going short, you will recall, means selling something you don't own. That would be larcenous were you not obligated eventually to buy it back —cheaper, you hope—to clear your account.) I called my broker and put in an order to short 1,000 warrants at 11¼. Only when that transaction was completed (for it's always trickier to short something than to buy it) did I buy an equal number of shares of Warner common stock.

If the stock is 55 or below on April 30, 1986, the warrants will expire worthless, which means I won't have to pay anything to buy them back and clear my account. I'll be allowed to keep the full 11¼ points on the warrant—$11,250.

If the stock is above 55, the warrant will have some value— but the more the better! Grab a pad and pencil and consider the possibilities.

Let's say the stock is 66. Well, the warrant will be 11 or so (as it entitles you to buy a $66 stock for $55), and I won't have any profit from having shorted it. But that's OK—I will have made 38 points on the stock. Thirty-eight thousand dollars! I *tremble* in anticipation.

For every point Warner is above $66, I will lose a point on the warrant but gain a point on the stock, and so still have a 38-point profit overall. What's more, the gain will be long-term, while any loss on the warrant will be short-term (gains and losses from short sales are always short-term), and that can work to my advantage.

If Warner is exactly where it was when I did all this—28¼— then I make nothing on the stock, but the warrants expire worthless and I get to keep $11,250.

If Warner is someplace between 28 and 55, I'll make someplace between 11 and 38 points.

Of course, should Warner slump to 3, say, I'd lose a lot more on the stock ($25,250) than I'd make on the warrants ($11,250). But you've got to take *some* risk if you want to join the Pepsi generation. (Another risk, please note, is that the company could unilaterally extend the life of the warrants.) Nor, should the stock fall, does anyone say I have to sell it. The warrants expire, but the stock lives on.

THE TWO-FOR-ONE REVERSE WARRANT HEDGE: MORE OF THE SAME

I was feeling quite pleased with myself for figuring all this out when I ran into Jeff Tarr. At Harvard, years ago, Jeff had launched Operation Match, the original computerized-dating service. Now he is one of Wall Street's most highly regarded arbitrageurs. We live in the same building, only he lives on a much higher floor. (The entire floor.)

"I've finally got one for *you*," I said, and I told my Warner story.

"Sure," he responded. "We've done a lot of that, only we figure you should be shorting two warrants for each share of the common. It's a two-for-one reverse warrant hedge."

I went home, took out my pad and pencil to see what would happen at various prices if I were to short *two* warrants for each share of the common stock, and then called my broker to short more warrants.

In mid-1984 the stock was down to 19, but the warrants, happily, had sunk to 1⅞.

ALA MOANA: TAKE A GAIN ON THE STOCK, REPORT A LOSS

Ala Moana would be worth mentioning even if it weren't a potentially great play, just for the volcanic passion of the name. But the idea was to buy the stock at 2½ and sit pat. Simple as that. Ala Moana Hawaii Properties, as it's formally known and traded on the New York Stock Exchange, is in the process of liquidating itself. Wiser minds than mine have guessed that the liquidating dividend will be in the neighborhood of $4—although wise minds, I cannot stress too forcefully, have been wrong before. They further guess that it will come sometime before the end of the century. Perhaps even before the end of 1984.

To turn $2.50 into $4 ain't hay, but what makes this play interesting, if it works, is that at the same time as one is turning $2.50 into $4, one may get to report a sizable *loss*. This is possible because: (a) The properties it's hoped will fetch $4 a share are on the books for a lot more; and (b) Ala Moana shares —never mind that they trade on the New York Stock Exchange —are not shares of stock but, rather, limited-partnership units. Ala Moana is not a corporation but a limited partnership. As such, profits and losses flow through to the partners.

It was a neat play, but for a rarefied crowd. The $4 might never materialize (although the first $1 has already been paid out). And the legal and accounting fees could be significant.

For Jeff Tarr, such expenses are justifiable. His group owns 890,000 shares.

PAN AM:
SHORT THE STOCK, BUY THE BONDS

It is February 1983 and Pan Am is desperate for cash to carry it through to summer. Some people are buying the stock at 5, hoping for a recovery. Others are buying bonds E. F. Hutton has concocted—"Pan American World Airways, Inc., 15 Percent Convertible Secured Trust Notes Due 1998." They pay 15 percent a year interest, are convertible into stock at $5.50 a share and are secured by a bevy of Boeing 747s. The smart money is buying the bonds and shorting the stock.

Roughly speaking:

If Pan Am should recover (which seemed doubtful in February 1983), the stock could soar—but the bonds, being convertible into the stock, would soar with it. A break-even.

If Pan Am limped along and the stock sat around 5, the bonds wouldn't move much either—but would be paying 15 percent for your trouble. Not bad.

If Pan Am went broke, the stock would collapse, yielding a huge profit to those who had shorted it—but the bond, secured by those 747s, might retain much of its value. Bingo!

The common thread in all of these plays is limited risk. His is a running, not a passing, game, Jeff Tarr says. Three yards at a time. (A friend who has run his $6,000 trust fund up to $800,000 in fourteen years puts it this way: "All I try to do is make 30 percent a year. Anything after that is gravy.") But the fellow I should really talk to about all this, Tarr says, is former MIT math professor Edward O. Thorp. Ed Thorp, Tarr says, *wrote the book* on this kind of thing.

ED THORP'S BOOK

Ed Thorp's book, coauthored by fellow math whiz Sheen T. Kassouf and published in 1967, was called *Beat the Market, A Scientific Market System*. One should, of course, be highly skeptical of books with such titles, but Thorp's previous book, in 1962, was called *Beat the Dealer*. It was the one that showed the world how to count cards at blackjack.

"Wall Street is a bigger game," Thorp grins, sitting at the conference table in his Newport Beach, California, office, "and you don't have to worry about anyone breaking your knees if you win." He and his partner in Princeton, James "Jay" Regan, manage a nine-figure sum for private clients. Since forming Princeton/Newport Partners in 1969, they've averaged nearly a 20 percent annual return, less their own hefty profit share. (Compounded at 20 percent for fourteen years, a dollar grows thirteenfold. Invested in the Standard & Poor's 500 index over the same period, with dividends, it would merely have tripled.)

Guided by a pair of Serious Computers, the partnership trades like crazy to exploit glitches in the market. Brokerage fees run into the millions each year. Some 90 percent of their trades succeed, Thorp says, albeit on a modest scale. A few succeed on an immodest scale.

RESORTS INTERNATIONAL: BUY THE WARRANTS, SHORT THE STOCK

In 1972, stock in badly troubled Resorts International was 8, and warrants that entitled you to buy it at 40 were, understandably, cheap. But 27 cents? Thorp's model, weighing the length of time to expiration, expected interest rates and the volatility of the underlying stock, told him the warrants were worth $4. He bought all he could—10,800 of them—for a total outlay, including commissions, of $3,200. But rather than risk even so modest a sum, he shorted 800 shares of the common stock to hedge his bet. Remember, we're talking arbitrage, not speculation.

A few months later, the stock fell to 1½, so Thorp covered his short for a profit that more than paid for the warrants—which he kept.

Years passed.

Around 1978, he began getting calls from people who wanted to buy his warrants. They were offering $3 and $4—not bad for 27-cent warrants—but by then, Resorts was trading around 15, and Thorp's model told him the warrants were worth $7 or $8. So he *bought more* (and began shorting the stock again as a hedge).

He ultimately sold his original 10,800 warrants, purchased at

27 cents, for $100 apiece. "All those guys in the Resorts casino counting cards," Thorp chuckles at the irony. "We found an even better way."

MARKET INDEX FUTURES:
SELL THE INDEX, BUY ITS COMPONENTS

When futures contracts were first offered on the Standard & Poor's 500, in April 1982, investors were able, in effect, to go long or short the whole market—all 500 S&P stocks at once. But especially at first, the prices at which those contracts traded were often a little out of whack.

If I were to show you a $5 bill and a roll of 100 20-cent stamps, you'd pretty quickly figure that the package was worth $25. You'd be unlikely to offer more; I'd be unlikely to accept less. But if I showed you 38,420 lire, 62 guilder, 2 million yen and some peso-denominated traveler's checks and offered you the right to buy the whole works six months from now, you might be less certain what to pay. And frankly, who would *care* if you paid a tiny bit too much? Ed Thorp's computer cares.

And Ed Thorp's computer was ready to run those calculations the moment S&P futures contracts began trading. Few other traders were quite so fast off the mark.

So from June to October 1982, Thorp's group busied itself selling (and buying) S&P futures contracts and buying (or selling) the stocks those contracts represented. The idea wasn't to guess which way the market was headed—quite the contrary. The idea was to exploit the inefficiencies of the marketplace. In effect, to buy $5 bills for $4.90 or sell them for $5.10.

This entailed truly extraordinary activity. Every time the command went out to sell overvalued S&P contracts, orders would also go out to buy corresponding numbers of shares of 265 different stocks. (Calculations showed that risk could be sufficiently reduced using 265 rather than all 500 of the stocks in the S&P 500.) The partnership was doing 700 trades a day at one point—generating more than 1 percent of the total New York Stock Exchange volume on some days—turning over, in all, something like half a billion dollars of securities over the four-month period. It meant tying up about $25 million of the partnership's capital and racking up monumental brokerage commissions. But the four-month profit came to $6 million.

The game petered out as other players wised up. Now $5 sells for so close to $5, it hardly pays to play.

BANCROFT CONVERTIBLE FUND: RAZZLE-DAZZLE

Can you stand one more?

Bancroft is a closed-end mutual fund—one of those rare mutual funds that, after it was sold to the public, closed its doors to future investment (most mutual funds will eagerly accept as much new money as people want to pitch into them). Its shares, representing tiny slices of the fund, trade on the American Stock Exchange.

In theory, if a fund's portfolio is worth $50 million and the fund is divided into 10 million shares, each of them should be worth $5—right? Typically, though, closed-end funds sell at a discount.

So, pleased at the thought of buying $5 bills for $4, Thorp and Regan went into the open market and from July 1977 through July 1978 accumulated 9 percent of all Bancroft's shares at a 20 to 25 percent discount from their net asset value.

To hedge against a general market decline, they sold short many of the very same securities Bancroft owned.

The thought was perhaps to persuade Bancroft management to convert itself to an open-end fund or to liquidate, either of which would allow shareholders to redeem their shares at full, *un*discounted value.

Meanwhile, a Florida bank holding company called Combanks had had much the same idea. It had purchased 11 percent of Bancroft (from Carl Icahn, yet another well-known arbitrageur). So in September 1978, Thorp and Regan graciously agreed to sell Combanks their shares—at a 10 percent discount to net asset value. Five-dollar bills they had bought for less than $4 each they were now selling for $4.50. Fat profit number one.

The following summer, they went back into the market and began buying up another 5 percent of Bancroft, still trading at a hefty 15 percent to 20 percent discount. They sold these shares not long afterward to financial conglomerate Baldwin United at a slim 5 percent discount. Fat profit number two.

Then Baldwin, which had also bought Combanks' holding and some others, got into a cash bind. So it sold the whole block of Bancroft—now fully 31 percent of all the shares outstanding—back to Thorp and Regan at an 11 percent discount. Five-dollar bills for $4.45.

Less than ninety days later, Thorp and Regan were successful in forcing Bancroft management, with which by then they had more than a little clout, to make a public tender offer for their shares at a mere 1 percent discount from net asset value. Fat profit number three.

Had all Bancroft shareholders tendered—which it would seem to have been unquestionably in their interest to do—Bancroft management would have had to sell off its portfolio, distribute the cash and find other work. Interestingly, few shareholders other than Thorp and Regan tendered their shares. This may have had something to do with the fact that, where most tender offers are advertised with blaring enthusiasm, Bancroft management chose to make this one . . . quietly. Managements are generally far more interested in their own welfare than that of their shareholders—particularly their smaller ones.

THE CHRYSLER PLAY:
BUY THE PREFERRED, SHORT THE COMMON

This was my other great idea. I never actually got around to doing it, but it did seem awfully smart at the time.

There was Chrysler in 1981, $6 a share and headed for zero, and there was Chrysler preferred, also $6 but a very different animal. The preferred stock came with a $2.75 dividend—never to be raised or lowered—and the promise that if Chrysler ever fell behind in paying that dividend, not a penny could be paid to the common-stock holders until every cent due the preferred shareholders was paid. At the time, about $5 in preferred dividends had been omitted, and more was accruing every quarter. My thought was to short the common stock and buy the preferred.

Two things could happen:

1. Chrysler could go bust. In that event, the creditors might eventually get some small portion of the money owing to them, but there would surely not be enough to pay everybody off and have anything meaningful left over for the common shareholders. So the common stock would trade at next to nothing. The preferred stock would also be worth next to nothing, except that in bankruptcy preferred stock gets in line ahead of common stock, so maybe it would be worth a little something after all. My gain from shorting the common stock should equal or exceed my loss on the preferred.

All in all, not a terrible prospect.

2. Chrysler could hang in there, catch an upswing in the economy and survive another cycle. How would the two securities act then?

Well, ultimately, the value in a common stock derives largely from the stream of dividends it will pay out over the decades. Yet before Chrysler could restore so much as five cents of the 10-cent-a-share quarterly dividend it had discontinued on the common in the summer of 1980, it would have to pay off the entire arrearage on the preferred stock, which would have been cumulating (as they say) inexorably at $2.75 per year.

So if Chrysler began to show marginal signs of health, the common stock might bounce a little (how high could it bounce under that Alpine debt, besieged by G.M. and Japan?), but the preferred might really mean something. There would be the prospect of a one-time payment of better than $11 a share (if it came, say, in December 1983) to clear up the arrearages, plus an additional $2.75 a year For the Rest of Time. Surely, under such circumstances, you'd have a valuable little piece of paper on your hands. Whatever it would be worth, it would be a heck of a lot more than the $6 you paid for it!

So what little you might lose covering your short in the common you would make up, very handily, on the profit and the dividends from the preferred. However well the common did, I figured—and I couldn't imagine it doing very well—the preferred would have to do better.

Obviously, two things were at work here to make my opportunity. The common was selling unrealistically high, at 6, bid up by unsophisticates excited by the charisma of Lee Iacocca and prone to invest with their hearts rather than their calculators; while the preferred was selling unrealistically low, dumped by the folks who ordinarily do buy preferreds—white-shoe types who were not about to scuff those shoes with an issue as scruffy as this one.

3. I had not considered the third possibility, which was that Chrysler would do brilliantly, pay off its government-guaranteed loan seven years early and show substantial signs of robustitude. As I write this, Chrysler preferred is up from 6 to 22⅝ (after having paid out $11.68 in accumulated dividends), which is the part I had hoped would happen—a huge, long-term capital gain, plus a huge, lump-sum dividend payment. What I did not expect was that Chrysler common would climb from 6 to 26. Even so, I would currently be ahead some $400,000 had I

only had the sense, and the dollars, to do this with, oh, say, 50,000 shares.

One could go on. Have we even mentioned options? Straddles? Spreads? No, we have not. Have we discussed arbitrageurs soaking up huge blocks of stock in takeover battles? Shares sold by people thrilled to get $57 for a stock that until Tuesday was $35, never mind that if the deal goes through they'd get $61? (The arbitrageur buys at 57 hoping for 61, or even more if the bidding heats up, a few weeks later.) No we have not! But this sort of thing is more fun to read about when the dollars involved are one's own. The important point in all this may be *not* that you or I should try playing these games, but that we should appreciate the kind of pros we're up against when we do.

Indeed, how *are* we to hold our own in the battle for financial survival (as it's been called)? Whom *can* we trust? Where *can* we turn? This is precisely the stuff—not all of it encouraging—of chapters 9 through 13. But first a word about money for those who haven't got any.

6

BORROWING IT
Getting Rich Risky

The general rule on borrowing money is not to. But there are times when it is unavoidable or even wise. The two questions to ask about any loan are its purpose and its cost. As with most things financial, prudence and common sense are all that are required to make a good decision. It doesn't take a genius to sense the difference between borrowing at 5 percent and borrowing at 20 percent; or between borrowing to buy a house, a car, and a vacation. A house maintains its value or may even appreciate; a car gradually depreciates; a vacation is gone the minute you return home to an even higher pile of bills.

It makes little sense for a young family to wait for a house until it can be bought for cash. An affordable mortgage is a sensible use of debt. But it *does* make sense to wait to take a trip. If you do, you have the fun and anticipation of saving up for it, and its cost is not inflated by finance charges. You are paying for it out of desire, not obligation. If you fly-now-pay-later, you could spend months saving up for a trip you've already taken. It's your choice: the carrot or the stick. (Needless to say—and here's where common sense comes in—if you can save a fortune by flying now, on some special fare, and if it won't take you long to pay off the debt, it could certainly pay to borrow to snag the bargain.)

There are millions of people for whom life is simply 18 or 20 percent more expensive than for everyone else. This is the premium they pay on almost everything they buy in order to be able to buy it now, on credit. Were they to scrimp and save for a year to get ahead of the game—I'm not saying it's easy— everything would forever after cost them 18 or 20 percent less.

This was not so important when inflation was running at double digits. In fact, for those who itemized their tax deductions, it often made sense to borrow at 18 percent—perhaps 10 percent after giving effect to the value of the tax deduction—and buy things they would otherwise have bought a year later for, say, 15 or 20 percent more.

But at least temporarily (and perhaps less temporarily than many people think), those days are past.

WHEN TO BORROW

• *If you don't need money, but wish to establish credit in case you ever do,* take out a small loan secured by a portion of your savings. Put the borrowed cash someplace safe, like the bank, and be sure to pay it back on time.

If you have $2,000 earning 10 percent in a savings account, your bank will likely lend you up to that amount at 11 or 12 percent. Such a loan serves no rational purpose, but this is the price you pay to prove your creditworthiness. An honest face is no longer enough.

• *If you need money for something you can comfortably afford but find yourself short of cash,* borrowing serves as a bridge. It carries you through until your tax refund arrives or your bonus comes through or your savings certificate matures.

One of the things many families can comfortably afford—but not all in cash—is a house.

• *If you need money for something you can barely afford but simply have to have.* Like a car.

• *If you can borrow for less, after-tax, than you can safely earn.* For example, many people can borrow against their life insurance policies for as little as 5 percent. If they buy long-term Treasury bonds that yield 12 percent, they will lock in a long-term profit from every dollar they borrow.

• *To fund a Keogh Plan or IRA.* The cost of borrowing is deductible, while the interest your IRA earns is sheltered from tax. More important, your IRA and Keogh contributions are themselves tax-deductible, even if you don't itemize. It would be a shame to miss out on that big deduction—and a more secure future—just because you were short of cash as the deadline drew near.

• *To start your own business.* Most new businesses fail. But if you want to break your back running a Takee Outee fast food franchise (which I seriously considered after I tasted Takee Outee teriyaki), or if you've come up with an idea for a new magazine on personal finance (just what the world needs—another magazine on personal finance), or if you've invented a process for converting weeds to whiskey—far be it from me to discourage you. Borrowing money to fund your own efforts is quite different from borrowing to invest in someone else's scheme. (At least you know you're not out to fleece yourself.) But unless you're extraordinarily confident of success, make every effort to finance your venture by taking on investors rather than personal debt.

WHEN NOT TO BORROW

When you don't have to. Indeed, the best way to "earn" 18 or 20 percent on your money, risk-free, is by not going into hock to a department store or bank credit card. Particularly if you don't itemize your tax deductions, and so can't lay off some of the cost on the government, it is folly to pay such rates if you can possibly avoid it. Yet many people keep money in a savings account, earning 5½ percent—which might net them only 4 percent after taxes—at the same time as they are paying 18 percent to buy on time. They are earning 4 cents on each dollar with their left hand while paying out 18 cents or more with their right—for a loss of 14 cents on every dollar they've borrowed.

Even if you do itemize your deductions, the only way it makes sense to borrow at 18 percent is if you have some risk-free way to earn *19 percent*.

It's true that to someone in the 50 percent tax bracket, borrowing at 20 percent is really like borrowing at only 10 percent —but so is *earning* 20 percent really like *earning* only 10 percent.

It's also true that there are two kinds of money your borrowed dollars can earn. If you borrow at 12 percent to earn 11 percent in dividends or interest, you will clearly come out behind. If you borrow at 12 percent to earn 11 percent in long-term capital gains, you will come out well ahead. The 12 percent you pay to borrow may actually be only 6 percent, after giving effect to the tax deduction (even less in states that have income taxes of their own), whereas the 11 percent you earn will not be taxed at all until you actually take your profit—be it on a home or a stock or some other asset—and then, after what may have been years of tax-free accumulation, only 40 percent of the gain (under current tax law) will be taxed.

This is a basic and powerful money angle for high-tax-bracket individuals, but it's not without risk. The 12 percent you *pay* is certain. The 11 percent capital appreciation you hope to earn (or 20 percent or 50 percent or whatever you're shooting for) is far less certain.

Say you borrow $200,000 to buy a $240,000 condominium in Aspen, as a young friend of mine did in 1980, knowing that prime properties can only appreciate each year. You pay $24,000 a year interest and get a great tax deduction. Then interest rates rise (up goes your variable rate mortgage) and down goes the market value of your property. After four years and $96,000 in interest, you sell the condo for $215,000, less 6 percent to the broker. So you're out $96,000 in interest (less whatever profit over expenses you may have earned renting it) and a further $38,000 in principal. The blow is softened by virtue of tax benefits, but it's a blow nonetheless.

Sure, the real estate agent will tell you the property will fetch $325,000 in four years—*easy*—in which case the numbers work out nicely . . . but it will be the rare real estate agent who backs that ready confidence with his or her own $325,000.

One old angle for playing this game involved borrowing money to buy soon-to-mature top quality bonds at a discount. Say the bond was issued at 4.5 percent in 1965 and was due to mature in thirteen months, in 1985. Say, further, that the bond is selling at 93 cents on the dollar. (No bond that yields a mere 4.5 percent is likely to sell for a full 100 cents on the dollar these days until it is mere seconds away from maturity.) You'd buy, say, $200,000 of the bonds on the thinnest margin you could (typically, your broker will lend you 70 percent for a corporate bond, 90 percent for a Treasury bond), and then wait for the bonds to mature.

The interest you paid to buy the bonds on margin was deductible. The interest you earned from the bonds (4.5 percent a year) is fully taxable. But the long-term capital gain you earned when each $930 bond was redeemed for $1,000 was only lightly taxed. And that is the aspect of this ploy that used to make it popular.

There were risks, but never mind all that—in 1984, after decades, Congress put a stop to the whole thing.

There are other angles. You can borrow to invest in research-and-development deals, almost all of which fail, or borrow to invest in syndicated real estate deals, almost all of which tack at least 15 percent onto the market value of the properties being syndicated (would you buy *your* house for 15 or 20 percent

more than it's worth?) You can borrow against the value of
your Treasury bills to buy, around June 28, puts and calls that
have at least six months and a day to run (the new long-term
capital gains holding period), planning to sell losers a day or
two *before* they go long-term, for a fully deductible (up to
$3,000) short-term capital loss this year, and winners a day or
two *after* they go long term, for a lightly taxed long-term capital
gain next year.* Your broker will be thrilled.

In short, if you're a high-income individual who knows what
he's doing, there's a place for borrowing to invest, in hopes of
trading deductible interest payments for only partially taxed
long-term capital gains. But if you've got one child, another on
the way and $63,000 in income—nothing to sneeze at, by any
means—the only place this is likely to make sense is in the
mortgage on your home.

WHERE TO BORROW

Borrow wherever the rate is cheapest. For a loan of any size,
talk to your bank, its competitors, knowledgeable friends, your
employer (some firms make low-interest loans to employees),
your credit union, if you're fortunate enough to belong to one,
and your accountant. If you're buying a car, talk to the auto
dealer. If you're buying a home, talk to your real estate agent
—and to the seller, who might be willing to take back a mortgage of his own.

If you own stocks or bonds, talk to your broker. Recently,
Sears was levying 21 percent interest on its charge card balances, while lending to clients of its stockbrokerage subsidiary,
Dean Witter, at a mere 12 percent. If you own cash-value life
insurance, talk to your insurer.

* But don't try to do this by buying puts and calls on the *same* stock, or on a
stock you already own in your portfolio, or by buying puts and calls on stock
indices, because the new law will trip you up.

If you are a student, talk to your financial aid office. If you are a veteran, you doubtless know to ask about VHA mortgages. If you are Brazil, talk to the IMF. Ordinarily, however, there are no magic sources of cheap money.

FINE POINTS

• Unless you're over fifty-five or in very poor health, don't take the credit life insurance option most lenders offer.

• Repay most loans as quickly as you can, but not low-interest loans (such as student loans) or most fixed-rate mortgages. A 9 percent fixed-rate mortgage is a treasure. Even a 12 or 13 percent fixed-rate mortgage is an asset, because it is so one-sided in your favor: if interest rates drop, you can always pay it off or refinance; but if interest rates should someday soar, the lending institution is stuck with you.

• The choice between fixed-rate and variable-rate mortgages is easy only if you know which way interest rates are headed— and no one does. Your decision thus depends on the specific alternatives you're offered and your own financial circumstances. You're safer with a fixed-rate loan, but it will cost more. My own feeling is that if you can't afford it, you probably can't afford the house.

• Beware gimmicky loans that start out cheap but have any of a number of fancy provisions that could come back to haunt you. You may be guaranteed, for example, that your monthly payments will rise by no more than 7.5 percent a year, warns *Newsweek* columnist Jane Bryant Quinn. "But here's the gimmick: the interest rate on your loan will rise to market levels, even though your payments are held down." So each month the interest you don't pay gets added back to principal. The increase in your monthly payments is limited, but the outstanding balance of your loan may grow bigger and bigger.

Before you commit to an adjustable mortgage, be sure you understand *exactly* how it works.

● Eschew thirty-year mortgages. You may be able to get a slightly lower rate on a fifteen- or twenty-year mortgage. But the main thing is that for a surprisingly small hike in your monthly payment you will save a fortune in interest.

Consider a $75,000 mortgage at 13½ percent. If you choose a thirty-year term, you'd pay $859 per month. On a twenty-year term, just $905. That's $46 a month more to save a decade of interest charges. (A savings of $91,944, to be exact.)

On a fifteen-year term the payment rises to $974, but you may be able to get half a point knocked off the interest rate, so payments would be just $949. That's 10 percent higher than with a thirty-year loan, but you'd own your home in half the time.

For high-tax-bracket individuals with great investment opportunities, thirty-year mortgages at today's rates may make sense. But for most people who can manage a shorter term—no.

● The below-market-rate auto loans car dealers offer from time to time are obviously attractive. But before accepting one, find out how much further the dealer could shave his price if you paid cash (and what values are available from competitors offering less generous financing).

● It would be great for rich folk if the interest on money borrowed to buy tax-free municipal bonds could be deducted. The idea would be to borrow from one's broker at 12 percent—the equivalent of perhaps 6 percent after tax—and earn *10 percent,* tax-free, from the bonds. In fact, the government has thought of this. The IRS disallows interest deductions incurred in connection with the ownership of tax-free bonds.

● But you *can* deduct interest incurred to buy utility stocks, the dividends from which are often partially tax-free (either through dividend reinvestment plans that convert ordinary income into long-term capital gains, or when the payouts are deemed a "return of capital"—ask your broker for details).

Having said this, I repeat: borrowing money to invest, even in something so stodgy as utility shares, let alone Hoo-Hah-Tronics or some jazzy tax shelter, is risky business.

THE PROBLEM

The problem with borrowing money is that as soon as one has, one inevitably begins to think of it as one's own. One becomes used to it, treats it like family, and may even come to resent or lose sight of the fact that it must all someday leave to visit someone else.

Borrowing is simple. Paying back's what hurts.

7

KEEPING IT

A Few Words on Taxes from a Man Who Knows

Somehow, in this doggy-dog world, you've made it. ("It's a dog eat dog world out there," I warned a six-year-old. "It's a doggy-dog world out there!" he giggled back gleefully for the rest of the evening, entirely missing my point.) You've found your niche or your gig or your calling, and it's making you two hundred thousand tamales a year. You and the President of the United States are in the same income bracket, only he earns his being President (you own a car wash), and he has to pay taxes. There are any number of tax-shelter promoters around who will tell you that you don't.

The minute you make some real money the battle begins. On one side is the IRS, which wants it; and on the other are the tax-shelter guys, who also want it. The object is for you to sneak across the battlefield with a little something intact. But it's not easy, because what do you know about modern warfare?

Listen to Buddy Hackett on why he went into the disastrous Home-Stake Oil tax shelter: "I haven't the vaguest idea. I just tell jokes. My lawyers and accountants look into these things and explain them to me in baby talk. If it sounds okay we go ahead." *

Two hundred thirty million Americans are subject to the Internal Revenue Code; a few thousand really understand it.

I went to see one of them.

Stuart Becker, forty-one, is six feet tall, two hundred twenty-five pounds (at least), grayish reddish blond and good-humored. He enjoys being Stuart Becker. He has two teenaged boys and a girl by his first and only marriage, now being litigated; a BMW, a 31-foot Aquasport and a weekend home in the Bahamas by virtue of his $250-plus-an-hour fees; an Italian girlfriend and real marble on the floor of his five-bathroom Sutton Place apartment. He's up at 6:45 every morning, walks to the 12,300-square-foot mid-Manhattan office that's home to thirty employees (marble in the lobby, teak ship's decking in his office), lunches at The Four Seasons every day, and leaves the office around 8:00, except Wednesdays, when he leaves early to drive to Long Island and visit his kids. (If you need to reach him, there's a phone in the car.) His own mid-six-figure income he shelters with oil and gas deals, leasing deals and real estate deals. He does pay some income tax—it's foolish not to, as he will explain—but he doesn't pay much. His hobbies are boating and fishing. His favorite toy is his Apple III personal computer. Favorite book: *From Those Wonderful Guys Who Gave You Pearl Harbor*. Favorite magazine: *Business Week*. Scotch: Dewars' White Label. (Really.) Quote: "The government ought to give me $3.5 million, tax-free, to spend a year helping them close loopholes." Boy, could he ever show them a thing or two, he says.

Becker's business is tax avoidance, the perfectly legitimate distant cousin to tax evasion (a crime). The former involves

---

* *Stealing from the Rich: The Home-Stake Oil Swindle,* David McClintick's excellent book, is the source of this quote and the two that follow.

ingenuity, the latter fraud. Sometimes the former involves a little of the latter, but that is a different story and not Stuart Becker's business. He plays by the rules of the most complicated game in the world, an intellectual challenge he clearly enjoys, and which annually nets his firm some $2.5 million in fees from some 600 clients. He is a former adjunct professor of taxation at New York University and a member of the executive committee of the tax division of the New York State Society of Certified Public Accountants.

This is, in other words, not your typical bright young man supplementing his income at H&R Block.

So here is what I learned: if you are one of the vast majority of taxpayers with no way to shelter your income beyond the standard ho-hum deductions and perhaps a Keogh plan, salary reduction plan or individual retirement account, you may be one of the lucky ones, after all. Because, Becker says, of the perhaps two million people entangled in tax-shelter deals, at least half probably shouldn't be in them. And even of those who should, a good many individuals—seemingly wealthy—are actually walking bankrupts, who in some cases are not even aware of it.

Count your blessings.

Barry Tarlow, Hollywood lawyer, on why *he* went into Home-Stake: "It's a desperate feeling when it gets to be December, especially if you're self-employed and you have all this money in the bank—fifty or a hundred thousand dollars—that will just go in taxes if you don't make some investment. It's like throwing it down a sewer."

Throwing it into a last-minute tax shelter can be even worse. Better to pay fifty or fifty-five cents in taxes than to lose the whole dollar. One of Becker's acquaintances says a tax shelter is "when one guy has a great idea and another has a lot of money and six months later their roles are reversed." But even if a tax shelter deal is sound from both a business and a legal standpoint, Becker says (and 95 percent of the deals Becker sees he rejects), investors can still get themselves into big trouble.

What many people don't understand is that a tax shelter is not some magic way to wipe out taxes. It is simply a way, if successful, of *deferring* taxes by shifting income from one year to some future year. The income you shield from taxes this year inevitably comes back to haunt you in some future year (although in some cases it can come back in the form of a capital gain, and thus be taxed at a lower rate). A tax shelter is not a way to make your tax liability disappear; it is a way to postpone it and invest Uncle Sam's tax dollars for your own benefit in the meantime.

This is fine if you invest Uncle Sam's dollars prudently. But what if you spend them? Or lose them? What do you do when the Internal Revenue Service comes for its money? Very loosely defined, the money you manage to slip by Uncle Sam with huge write-offs in one year, but which he comes after sooner or later, is called recapture.

"The problem here," says Becker, "is how many people do you know who, if they've deferred twenty-five thousand dollars in taxes, take the twenty-five thousand dollars and put it away to pay the recapture? They spend it! I mean, it just goes. Okay? Of all my clients I have just one who takes the tax savings from these kinds of deals and puts them into municipal bonds, waiting for the recapture to come [but meanwhile earning tax-free interest on the government's money].

"There are guys out there who have sheltered so much that quite honestly, on a pure balance sheet basis, if you include their deferred tax liability, they're bankrupt. There's no way on earth they can pay it off. So when that income finally has to be declared, and the taxes on it paid, they will borrow and steal— or else go into another tax shelter. And if they do that, all they will be doing is creating a rolling ball that just gets bigger and bigger and bigger."

Or look what some sad souls do. They may be earning $40,000 a year, and through some tax shelter or other, manage to shift $10,000 from this year's tax return to next year's. They might have saved $3,000 on their tax bill by declaring $10,000 less income this year. But because the income tax is graduated, that same $10,000 added to next year's income might add an extra $4,000 in taxes, and thus actually increase the tax bill.

Only individuals in the 50 percent tax bracket should consider tax shelters—and only for that portion of their income actually taxed at the 50 percent rate. Becker fairly sniffs at the hypothetical advertising executive I asked him about who earns a hypothetical $75,000 a year (by most standards, not sniffing money). "Bear in mind," he says, "that if his total income is seventy-five thousand dollars, his taxable income, after deductions, is probably around sixty, if that. So, assuming he's married and filing jointly, he's only in the 38 percent bracket.

"Philosophically, it is a question of how far you want to shelter. I have many clients who insist on sheltering down to zero. I think that's wrong. [Are we about to get a little moralizing?] Because when you look at it long term, on the assumption that one way or another your tax-shelter deductions will become income in the future, why write off at 20 or 30 percent what you are going to recapture at 50 percent a few years down the road? [Apparently not.]"

To be sure, many deals are structured so that the income you receive, if you ever do, is partially free of tax. Oil and gas revenues still enjoy a depletion allowance; real estate and research-and-development deals are structured to return (at least in part) lightly taxed long-term capital gains. But if you do any of these deals in a really big way, at least a little of the fun may be spoiled by the Alternative Minimum Tax (talk to your accountant); and if you *don't* do these deals in a really big way, well, it's a little like the difference between buying retail (in this case, say, $5,000 units) versus wholesale (say, $150,000 units).

"Most good deals won't even consider investments of less

than twenty or twenty-five thousand dollars," says Becker. And why should they? If you had a really good deal, would you go to the trouble of splitting it into five thousand slices, or would you just get together a handful of well-heeled friends and acquaintances? You'd go for the more bothersome wide distribution only if you think the well-heeled, savvy crowd is too smart to go for it. The recent film production syndications, where you put up $5,000 for a tiny share in a basket of Major Motion Pictures, are a good example. Lots of fun and public appeal; not too many tax attorneys trying to get their own money into the deal.

Just about anything can be a tax shelter—a macadamia nut or avocado farm, an apartment building or shopping center, an oil well or coal mine, a boxcar or barge or towboat or grain elevator—so long as it is something that requires an initial investment that is largely deductible. When that investment begins to pay off, if it does, your investment is recouped (and the taxes are then due on the portion you deducted)—plus a profit, if you're lucky.

What juiced these deals up so much in the past, and still does in real estate, is the "nonrecourse" loan, by which you could write off from your income four or five times as much money as you actually invested. The tax savings were so great it didn't matter if the investment proved to be totally worthless—as most did.

By way of illustration, Becker describes the phenomenon of spaghetti Westerns, the old cowboy movies made in Italy that would be dubbed in English and shipped over here. American "investors" would pay, say, $1,025,000 for such a film— $25,000 in cash, plus a nonrecourse note for $1 million. That note would be paid off with proceeds from the film only. If the film made no money (as everyone knew it wouldn't), then the noteholder would not have recourse against the investor. But he never really expected any of the note to be paid off anyway.

"You showed the film three times," Becker explains. "You

took in four thousand dollars in box office revenue, you put it back in the can, up on a shelf, and wrote off your million dollars as a tax loss." Even though you had only put in $25,000, you got to take a tax deduction that could save you upwards of $500,000. "Then ten or fifteen years down the road, when the note came due, that's when you had your tax liability to face." (This is because the IRS figures that not having to pay off a $1 million debt is like receiving $1 million in income—and that's when it comes to recapture the taxes you deferred.)

Because many of these deals were made in the mid-seventies, while they were still marginally legal, many of the notes have not yet come due. When they do, some wealthy people are going to find themselves in a tight place.

Becker sees three scenarios for the thousands of individuals he reckons have recapture clouds of one sort or another hanging over their heads.

Some will roll over as much of the taxable income as they can into new tax shelters—although Congress and the IRS keep narrowing the field. Then they will grit their teeth and pay taxes on the rest.

Some will switch accounting firms and forget to mention that they ever went into these deals or took the fat initial write-off. Because it audits returns just one year at a time, the IRS is not well organized to follow a multiyear tax shelter deal.

And the third group? "In a few years," says Becker, "I see people—no, not jumping out of windows, but heading to those countries that do not have extradition treaties with the U.S. vis-à-vis tax evasion. I think people are going to reach a point where there's no way out except to leave. You're talking about huge amounts of money with some of these people."

Except in real estate, Congress has ruled out the use of non-recourse loans. The only way to deduct more than you invest is to be genuinely liable for the difference. (In the case of that spaghetti Western, an extra $1 million.) It's not uncommon now to hear, "Well, the prospectus *says* you're liable for the additional $80,000, but believe me, you won't have to pay it. We just put that in to make it deductible." Beware that sort of statement, because in tax shelters even more than most things, whatever can conceivably go wrong, will. If you sign a personal note for $80,000, the chances are good you will have to come up with that $80,000, whatever the salesman may tell you.

One participant in a Becker-recommended barge deal (you buy the barges and lease them out) says it's been a disaster. "We were never supposed to have to put in more money, but we've already had to put in an extra $18,000 per unit." He says Becker's been great at filing his returns and defending him in audits, but terrible in evaluating and recommending shelters. Another client says just the reverse.

It's a tough business. Any tax accountant or tax attorney is likely to be blamed for deals that go sour or audits that go poorly—and there's no way for all to go well.

One thing a reputable practitioner like Becker *can* be relied upon to do is to avoid "abusive" tax shelters. Like the mail-order ministries that, for $30, ordain you and encourage you to deduct all your living expenses as contributions to the church. Or the deals where you buy 5,000 bibles at $2 apiece, say, and turn around and donate them at their "full retail value" of $8.95. Or any other deal created solely to avoid taxation. The IRS has been going after abusive shelters in a serious way. Yet the desire for tax shelter is so great, and the slice to the promoters so fat, that even the bad deals get done.

There are reputable deals, reputable promoters and legitimate ways to defer and whittle away huge tax bills. What's more, most legitimate tax shelters are tax-favored for a reason, and not just to make the rich richer, even if Congress's reasoning sometimes goes awry. We do want to encourage capital investment and investment in research and development. We do want to spur the restoration of historic buildings and the building of low-income housing and the discovery of oil and gas. But prospects are advised to investigate any deal very deliberately, with the best available tax counsel. Those who can't afford such counsel—which is to say, most of us—probably do not have the kinds of tax bills for which shelters make sense in the first place.

And two more caveats:

● Accountants and advisers frequently stand to earn fat commissions from the deals they put you into. Under such circumstances, it can be hard for them to be objective. (Becker says that when a commission is available he always takes it—and rebates it to the client.)

● You can't make money by losing money. Only deals that would be at least marginally attractive *without* their tax benefits are worth investing in.

"You know the best tax shelter?" asks yet another Home-Stake investor. "Don't make any money!"

8

SPENDING IT
Let's Discuss My Toys

Well, I'm sorry, I do make money—more in a single month, I
don't mind telling you, than most men dream of making in a
week—and, although some of my friends would say otherwise,
I don't mind spending a little of it. (Most I throw down the tax-
shelter rat hole.) Occasionally I even go to disgusting excess,
which I justify by the Spartan fact that I own no car.

If you have any breeding at all you will skip this chapter. It's
personal and nobody's business but my own. But if you are the
leering, peeping, loitering type—the type that reads *People*
magazine and that dallies over the *Shaper Image* catalog—wel-
come.

Every year I take what I save by not owning a car and buy
myself a toy. As it now costs $350 a month just to garage a car
in some of New York's pricier undergrounderies, I can afford
some pretty fancy toys. There's the six-foot TV, the three-inch
TV, the photocopier, the computer, the other photocopier, the
other computer, the microwave oven, the video tape recorder,
the Florida condo, the . . .

I went through a phase like this once before, albeit on a more
modest scale, directly out of college. I had giant inflatable whiskey bottles and toothpaste tubes, a three-foot lava lamp (which

I had bought for my parents' anniversary, but which they had refused), a Foosball game, light boxes filled with blinking Christmas tree lights and a gizmo from the Museum of Modern Art gift shop with red velvety fluid inside that swirled in wonderful patterns when you jiggled it. I had three phosphorescent balls. (Shut off the lights and juggle them, or put them inside your T-shirt to give yourself knockers that glow in the dark.)

I was young. I was foolish. I've grown up.

Executive Teddy Bear

I assume you have one of these, too, only yours may not have a tail you pull to crank up a little phonograph inside that says, "You're on your way to the top!" It also says, "There is *nothing* you can't do," harkening back to the old Henry Ford adage, "Whether you believe you can do a thing or not, you're right."

On rare occasion it will blurt out: "You're a winner, Teddy knows."

Gold Atmos Clock

This doesn't work very well, but it looks great on the mantel above my fireplace, which doesn't work at all. They say even a broken clock is right twice a day, but that's not true. One that runs a few minutes fast, like mine, can be wrong for months.

Black Knight Pinball Game

I saved a fortune buying this Black Knight pinball machine, because I had gone downtown planning to buy a Pac-Man ($2,600 plus tax). The salesman said Pac-Man was no longer available, and that the "Super Pac-Man" they were selling wasn't much of a game. "Don't waste your money," he said. ("But I *want* to waste my money," I said.) He seemed content

to let me walk out of the store empty-hearted, but I pressed
him. "What do you have that *is* good?" (It all looked good to
me: arcade games of every variety, pinball machines around
the block.) He led me to the Black Knight and let me have it—
a floor model—for about half what it was worth.

This sucker, in case you've never played it, takes quarters
and Susan B. Anthony dollars (which *do* look exactly like quarters, incidentally—was *that* ever dumb!) and is worth every
penny you put into it. It shouts at you, laughs derisively at your
mistakes and features a duplex playing field and magnets you
can activate to save balls from going down the gutters. And it
lights up like a Christmas tree when in the course of a single
turn you pop three balls into a sort of holding area up near the
top, whereupon all three are released for simultaneous play.
They do everything but glow in the dark.

Pig Mask

I always hated Halloween until I found this mask, stuck some
Press-Type dollar signs on it, slapped on my tux and started
going to parties as a capitalist pig. I still hate Halloween, but
less.

New York Stock Exchange Dart Board

I don't actually use this to pick stocks, but often should have.

Juke Box

My plan had been to buy a used one. It was the colors I
couldn't resist. A Mystic 478 by Rock-ola, it keeps track of
which songs are most frequently requested ("Dim All the
Lights," Donna Summer; "God Bless America," Elvis Pres-
ley); it starts flashing BONUS! when it's been neglected for a
while; it can really wake up the dead.

Kroytype Headline Writer

"Can I ask you something?" the young salesperson said hesitantly, when she had finished demonstrating this Kroytype headline maker and haggling over the number of free typewheels she'd throw in with the purchase.

"Sure," I said.

"What are you going to *use* this for?"

It is a question I've been asked frequently since, particularly as it remains where she demonstrated it, on my dining room table; and it is a question that anyone with any imagination should be able to answer with ease. I make headlines with it! Why, sure! If someone is coming over who I feel should have a name tag—out one pops. If some six-year-old friend is turning seven (a lot of my friends are turning seven because a lot of my former classmates are turning thirty-seven), I can dash off something impressive.

Mainly though (as I explained to the gentleman from the Internal Revenue Service), I use it to spiff up my memos and proposals with typeset-quality headlines.

Six-Foot Pencil

For when I have something really big to say.

Rubber Feet

These milk chocolate squares are actually rubber coasters to keep sofa legs from scuffing the floor. I keep them in a dish on the mantel. First time visitors rarely notice, but there are teethmarks in some of them.

Perpetual Motion Solar Bicycle

This is a six-inch solar-powered bicycle. When you shine a light bulb on it, a little man starts peddling for dear life. My plan is to hook him up to a generator that will power the light, my refrigerator, dishwasher and air conditioners.

Ginzu Knives

I didn't need these, but the TV offer was irresistible. What would you pay for all these knives that will slice steel like butter, the man asked. A hundred bucks? Two hundred? But hold on! What if we threw in this cheese chopper and this peppercorn cutter and this lampshade? *Now* what would you pay? *But hold on!* Look at this hatchet and this apple corer— *NOW WHAT WOULD YOU PAY?!* Eight hundred dollars? A thousand?

I have to tell you that my ginzu knives really are sharp, and that if I needed them, they would certainly have been a bargain at $19.95, which is the incredible price, if memory serves, at which all this cutlery became mine.

Neon Sign

I don't know if it's really neon or not, but it's the kind you see in bank windows with a continuous message looping through it. 90-DAY C.D.'s . . . 10.5 % !!! . . . HAVE A NICE DAY.

Mine stores thirty different messages, is a cinch to "program," and allows you to designate light face, bold face, upper case, lower case, the date and time (which it keeps current), and different marching orders for the letters. They can "walk on" from left to right, roll up from the bottom or roll down from the top, "wipe left," wipe right, flash on, flash off, blink—wait till you see it.

They don't have stuff like this in Bulgaria.

Huge Light Bulb

This is the largest light bulb I own. It was given to me by a fellow at an ad agency who thought it might fit my decor. It may work, but none of my sockets is big enough to find out.

New Yorker Cartoons

If you like a *New Yorker* cartoon, you can rip it out and frame it. For another few hundred dollars, you can buy the original and frame *it*. Collect what you like, art experts are always advising, so that's what I've done.

One of my favorites is titled, "Man with a Clear Conscience," by an artist named Barsotti. It shows a businessman sitting behind his desk in shirtsleeves, one finger on the intercom. "Mike Wallace to see you, sir," his secretary is saying through the squawk box. "Terrific!" says the man with a clear conscience. "Send him right in."

Floppy Diskette

A little man named Monty lives on this diskette. Monty plays Scrabble. Monty uses words like aa, ae, aas (the plural, apparently, of aa) and English renderings of all the letters of the Greek and Hebrew alphabets. Monty is a pain in the aas.

Incredibly Loud Shirt

I actually bought this shirt, but have never worn it seriously. Whenever I give a party and put a coat rack outside my door, I put this shirt on the first hanger to break the ice.

Garrett Morris

I know what this all brings to mind. It brings to mind that famous skit on "Saturday Night Live" in which Garrett Morris played the leader of a terribly poor African country—remember?—and appealed to us, the viewers, to send his desperate countrymen the electric fondue makers he knew we all had gathering dust up on a shelf in our closets.

Well, I have this to say about that. In the first place, I have no electric fondue maker. In the second, where can I get one?

SOURCES OF WISDOM

Never let a man jeopardize a fortune that he has earned in a legitimate way, by investing it in things in which he has no experience.

—P. T. Barnum

9

BROKERS
Meet Olumba Olumba Obu

The way to be very, very wealthy, someone wrote, is to be very, very, very rich. Short of that—far short—there are investment books and the business press and annual reports and investment letters and the Financial News Network, of which more in the chapters that follow; and there is Olumba Olumba Obu. But the first place the novice might turn to get rich is to a pro. A broker. For us, getting rich is merely a wish. For him, it is a calling.

Browsing through the collection of nineteenth-century advertising posters at the New-York Historical Society, with its ads for the bicycle ("an ever-saddled horse that eats nothing") and for Dr. John Wesley Kelly's Diamond Pectoral ("a sure, pleasant and safe remedy for all diseases of the throat and chest," pictured in a sweet family scene titled *Mother is Saved!*), one comes to a poster celebrating the nation's centennial. Dominating the poster is a prosperous farmer with his plow and horses. Beneath him, the banner I FEED YOU ALL! Framing the farmer are his countrymen, with banners of their own. There are the soldier (I FIGHT FOR ALL), the merchant (I BUY AND SELL FOR ALL), the clergyman (I PREACH FOR ALL), the doctor (I PHYSIC

YOU ALL), the lawyer (I PLEAD FOR ALL) and the stockbroker—
I FLEECE YOU ALL.

The artist just couldn't resist.

A lot of barbs have been aimed at stockbrokers since then,
but you'll find none of them here. Oh, sure, they smell funny
and would sell their moms for a dollar, but I'm not going to get
into all that, because almost none of it is true. (The smell comes
from handling county sewage bonds.)

The fact is that brokers, particularly since the prolonged
shakeout of the seventies, are for the most part a well-trained,
well-intentioned, hard-working and professional crew. The fact
also is that, on average, there is very little they can do to enrich
you that you could not do as well or better yourself (but that's
not their fault). And there's always the chance you will find the
outstanding, exceptional, far-above-average broker who can.

In 1981, there were 56,000 active brokers in the U.S.; by the
end of 1982, 64,000—and the great bull market had barely
begun. By now, the ranks have surely swelled beyond 70,000,
which means that with perhaps 20,000 new brokers all told in
the past few years, the phone has been ringing off the hook.
Twenty thousand brokers starting fresh and looking to sign up
200 or 300 clients each (graduates of E. F. Hutton's impressive
four-month training program are expected to sign up twenty
new accounts a month) may at first make sixty cold calls a day.
Some make far more. So you're talking maybe 300 million cold
calls a year. Which wouldn't be so bad, except that far from
being spread over the entire adult population, two calls apiece,
most of the calls are made to a relative handful of attractive
prospects.

The first thing you want, after you pass the six-hour "Series
7" exam that qualifies you to be a broker, is lists. People to
call. Some leads may be provided by your firm, but the freshly
matriculated broker will be encouraged to obtain or compile his
own lists as well. Hence the classified ads in *Registered Repre-
sentative* (the trade magazine that is to brokers approximately

what *Life Insurance Selling* is to life insurance salesmen) pitching lists of "42,000 casino 'credit-rated' gamblers. All have phone numbers. . . ."

Other available lists include aircraft owners, aircraft pilots, dentists, dentists who are heavy investors, Arabs who gamble and invest, cattle breeders, female investors, gold buyers and seminar attendees, investors who are known art lovers, investment-book buyers, investors concerned about inflation, Jewish investors, people with large deposits in savings accounts, high-value-home owners, Mexican-gold buyers, millionaires, investors in limited partnerships, psychiatrists, teachers who buy loaded mutual funds (i.e., dumb teachers), wealthy ranchers and farmers who invest, and ultrawealthy Americans. Given that the average psychiatrist is an ultrawealthy American millionaire concerned about inflation, with a high-value home, large savings deposits and a love of art—not to mention Jewish—one can imagine the volume of cold calls he must fend off in the course of a day.

We like to think of brokers as great stock pickers, and a handful are. Most spend very little time picking stocks. They are primarily engaged in selling new accounts and, as their book of business builds, servicing old ones. Listen to Ken Catanella, of E. F. Hutton's Philadelphia office, in a video-taped address viewed by thousands of brokers (not just Hutton's) across the country: "You must firmly believe and you must take the oath," he says, "that none of you are truly financial analysts. I know that I am not an analyst. *I am a salesman.* I look like a salesman, I dress like a salesman, I talk like a salesman. I am a salesman for the firm."

Catanella signed up an astounding 650 new accounts his first year with Hutton (previously, he had been with Paine Webber and then with Shearson, in Indiana). In his second year, 1981, he generated $1,100,000 in commissions for the firm, or about six times the average.

Very much a salesman, he exhorts his fellow brokers to

"throw away all the negative vibes you had when you walked into this room. And you know exactly what I mean. No more problems with the margin clerk, no more arguing with the office manager—you name it, it has to stay outside. The stock that research gave you at 40 that's now 20—leave it out there. I can't help you with that, and neither can anybody else. Open up now, and let me come in."

The three things that make someone a big producer, Catanella advises, "are, one, he must be hungry—hungry as hell."

"Two, he must be professional. We are not used-car salesmen in this business."

"Three, he absolutely must be dedicated. Dedicated means reading, studying, coming to conferences like these."

Not all brokers think of themselves as salesmen, and even the ones who do would just as soon *you* didn't think of them that way. As Catanella sees it, the smart salesman today needs a subtler pitch. "Asset allocation, not selling! You sell nothing! You asset allocate. Some real estate, some oil and gas, some utilities under dividend reinvestment, some growth stocks—you asset allocate, and for the first time in your client's life, somebody has shown him a plan."

Contrast that with the old-fashioned approach, still standard, that Catanella calls the influence sale.

"It's the carrot sale—the probing, teasing sale, where the investor really might not understand the product, but you cajoled him and you eased him into saying yes to it—that is not a comfortable sale as far as I'm concerned. I consider the client my equal. I like to educate the client. I feel very comfortable with that not only when I'm right but when I'm wrong."

Catanella thinks most investors consider their portfolios hobbies. "Once you convince them that you do the business not as a hobby but as a *war,* that it's your *life-blood,* that your family *depends* on it, your firm has *pride* in it, I feel that they will feel that they do need the assistance of a professional." Even if he is just a salesman and does have 649 other accounts to worry about at the same time.

Space precludes touching upon all of Catanella's sales theories: radio is more effective for brokers than newspaper advertising; cold calls are a waste of time; hire a high school girl to take down names from building directories; do all your mailings on parchment; seminars are great. But what the thousands of brokers who heard his talk didn't know, and what may be the tiniest bit embarrassing, is that—if the current set of plaintiffs in federal court is to be believed—"defendant Catanella took on more customers than he could possibly handle on a responsible basis; directed that unauthorized transactions be made for [their accounts] . . . repeatedly churned accounts so as to generate commissions to himself and Hutton; engaged in margin and options trading without disclosing the risks or costs"; and just was not what you'd call a square-shootin' guy. Hungry as hell, to be sure, but not a dedicated professional.

Of course, it's all well and good for a bunch of disgruntled customers to make accusations. Catanella denies them. But what keeps a layman from accepting his denial *entirely* at face value—and what makes Hutton's decision to hire and promote him telling—is Judge Cale J. Holder's opinion in a *previous* set of lawsuits (not the current ones, at this writing still pending) back in Indiana. "Mr. Catanella was guilty of intentional misconduct," the judge found in 1979. Punitive damages might well have been called for, he said, on top of the several hundred thousand dollars of compensatory damages he awarded, the judge noted; only under Indiana law you can't sock a guy with punitive damages if he's subject to criminal prosecution, and Catanella would have been subject to criminal prosecution had the statute of limitations not run out.

There was more than one plaintiff in the case, more than one defendant (Catanella had worked for both Shearson and Paine Webber) and more than one charge, but a few snippets from the opinion are worth quoting:

"The defendants knew that a commodities account was not in Mr. Brown's best interest. . . ."

"Mr. Catanella and [Paine Webber] by engaging in the found manipulative, deceptive and fraudulent acts, devices, schemes, contrivances and artifices defrauded and deceived Mrs. Aikman . . ."

"Mr. Brown in April of 1973 notified Mr. Catanella to sell all securities in his commodities account at [Shearson] and further notified [him to stop trading]. Mr. Catanella and Shearson disregarded Mr. Brown's notification and continued to make unauthorized and excessive purchases of commodities [for another four months] . . . for the purpose of generating unauthorized and excessive commissions."

Now here's the one I love:

"Mr. Catanella's and Paine Webber's bad judgment visited upon the Browns rose to a crescendo when Paine Webber sent its 'tax-shelter expert' and Mr. Catanella to interest Mr. Brown in investing in 'tax shelters,' even though they knew before they visited Mr. Brown that Mr. Brown was not in a 50 percent tax bracket and his losses in the stock market and in his farm operations gave him no tax to shelter."

But let's return the floor to Catanella and his 1982 videotaped address to brokers: "Credibility. How do you get it? You're gonna have to work extra to gain credibility. I don't care how you get it; I will tell you the areas that I think you should be involved in to get it. I think you should write a local article, I think you should try and do a talk show, I think you should try and do a market report. . . ."

Credibility. I don't care how you get it. It reminds me of George Burns's wonderful line about honesty. "The main thing about acting," he said, "is honesty." Long pause. "If you can fake that, you've got it made."

All brokers are not from one mold—far from it. The other man on the video tape was Leo Shear, a complete contrast to

Catanella, not nearly so dapper or self-assured. In 1962, Shear went to Wall Street from Dun & Bradstreet, where he had been a credit and financial reporter. His first full year as a broker, he grossed $12,000 in commissions. "I am not a salesman myself," he says, "or at least I do not consider myself as such." And yet he has become the largest producer on Long Island. (If you are wondering what it is exactly that brokers "produce," you are not seeing things from the firm's perspective. Brokers produce commissions.)

Shear would find one stock he really believed in and push it to anyone who would listen. Some went down; most, especially in the sixties, went up. And when they did go up, he wouldn't sell them. That might have generated commissions, but it would also have generated taxes for his clients. And as long as a winner was in the account, he looked good. Many of his clients were willing to refer new prospects, whom Shear diligently pursued. "From one lead in Rutland, Vermont," he says, "I now have between thirty and forty accounts up there. I've lost track of the number. I probably do more business than the local stockbroker."

He was handed a dormant account from a broker who'd quit, an account in Amherst, Massachusetts, that contained—are you ready?—eight shares of stock. He called the client "and got into a little discussion." That account subsequently referred fifteen others.

Shear is slow but steady. He says, and you believe him, "You should never recommend a stock because there's a large commission or the firm is pushing it. You should recommend it because you sincerely believe you are doing right for the client. The fact that there's a larger commission credit to a particular item is one that I find obnoxious. You sell a municipal bond not because there's a thirty-dollar credit instead of a ten-dollar credit; you sell the bond because you believe that product is right. And I stress that point because when you get through with all of this, you've got to live with yourself."

Most brokers would echo that sentiment wholeheartedly. But it's one thing to echo a sentiment and another always to resist temptation. And the temptation is always there. When in 1984 Smith Barney—the John Houseman firm—had several hundred thousand shares of a stock called Cordis to sell for a client at 15, and offered its brokers a special $1 credit per share to sell them, all the shares got sold at 15. Ten days later the stock was $9\frac{3}{8}$.

There's simply a lot more hucksterism in stockbroking than the big wire houses would have you know. (Even venerable Lehman Bros., whose clientele is largely institutional, had a cadre of high-powered retail telephone salesmen long before it merged into Shearson/American Express. "Our gorillas," a friend there affectionately calls them.)

Chances are, when your broker calls from Prudential-Bache's Phoenix office to suggest that you invest in the Prudential-Bache Research Fund, he won't tell you that there's a contest on in the office and that he and his fellows stand to win weekends for two at a resort. That is not to say the fund won't be terrific—who knows? Thus far it's down 15 percent (plus a redemption charge)—or that brokers foisted it upon even a single client to whom it was unsuited. It is merely to note the temptation. Prudential's Phoenix office sold $5,600,000 of the fund in a month.

In 1982, according to a broad survey conducted by the Securities Industry Association, the average broker grossed $164,000 in commissions and got to keep just over 40 percent of it: $67,000. Well, it's a living. Weed out from the survey brokers in training and it's an even slightly better living. In 1983, it was a better living still. Paine Webber's 3,800 brokers averaged around $95,000 apiece. For its 5,500 brokers, Hutton projects average pay of around $125,000 for 1985.

In addition to pay, there are perks (which tend to be skimpy), sales support and incentives. According to *Registered Repre-*

sentative, Hutton spends about $15 million a year on trips and contests.

Robert Hughes, manager of Mosely Hallgarten's New York office, prefers to emphasize new-account generation over sales when he runs a contest. "If you stress gross production," he told *Registered Rep,* "then you may induce someone to do something he shouldn't."

But most contests are won by selling.

And there's more than ever to sell. As banks and brokerage houses and life insurers encroach increasingly upon one another's turfs, "the traditional mandate to sell stocks," in the words of the *Wall Street Journal,* "has been supplanted by a new rallying cry: Capture assets."

Mrs. P (as we'll call her) is a sixty-eight-year-old widow who had $47,000 in a Merrill Lynch money-market fund. Her broker earned nothing from all those captured assets. (Merrill has since begun paying its brokers a sliver of money-market balances.) Being an enterprising fellow, and one of the more senior in the office, he called Mrs. P periodically to suggest that she switch her cash into one of Merrill Lynch's Ginnie Mae funds. Ginnie Maes (short for G.N.M.A., Government National Mortgage Association) are pools of government-insured mortgages. To understand fully the dynamics of the G.N.M.A. market takes a patient and agile mind, so it is easier to say simply (if you're trying to sell it) that the fund is completely safe—the U.S. government stands squarely behind these mortgages—and that the yield is about 12 percent instead of the 9 percent Mrs. P was earning. What's more, you can even write checks against the fund, just like a money-market fund! The two things Mrs. P's account executive did not tell her in the several calls he had to make before he finally persuaded her to switch were, first, that 3.9 percent of her $47,000 would immediately be syphoned into Merrill Lynch's pocket (the broker would get about $525 of that), and second, that her remaining $45,167 would fluctuate in value in response to market forces. Over the short term (which is something to consider when you're sixty-eight), it could go down.

And did.

A Merrill Lynch broker who refused to sell the G.N.M.A. product says, "These things were made to look just like money-market funds. Very clever from a marketing point of view. You can get paid monthly or, if you really want to complicate your life, reinvest the income from the fund. *Then* the monthly statements you get become *completely* incomprehensible. The check-writing feature they threw in to make it look even more like a money-market fund is crazy, because you are, in essence, taking a 3.9 percent bath every time you write a check."

The product is so complicated, the statements so unfathomable and the ranks of unhappy customers so large, this Merrill Lynch vice-president claims, Merrill had to put out a thirty-page memo to help brokers understand it. (The memo—marked FOR INTERNAL USE ONLY; DO NOT DISTRIBUTE—actually runs eleven pages. It does seem longer.)

In short, there is a big difference between being a successful broker, like Mrs. P's, and being a successful client. One broker who earned $500,000 in 1983 buying and selling stocks for his clients has *never* bought stocks for himself. "I'm no fool," he laughs, only half-kidding.

(If you do have a serious problem with a broker, it may not take twenty years and half a million dollars in legal fees to resolve it. Call the New York Stock Exchange to ask about the binding-arbitration service it offers. In relatively small disputes, you may not even need a lawyer. What will help—few of us think to keep them until it's too late—are notes on the instructions you've given your broker and notes on the advice and information he's given you.)

There is a strong case to be made that the overwhelming majority of brokers will do no better investing your money than you would do throwing darts at the stock pages. Therefore, if you trade with any frequency or in any volume, you should avail yourself of the services of a discount broker and save yourself a pile of money on commissions. Or buy shares in a prudently selected no-load mutual fund or two and get professional management of your money without nearly the paperwork and worry of buying and selling stocks yourself—see chapter 14.

But if you think discount brokers lack cachet and mutual funds are too tame (they're not! You can lose a bundle in mutual funds, too!), or if it is the buying and selling and paperwork that you *like*—if, that is, you are looking for a coach and confidant or for someone to blame or complain to, where do you look?

One sensible suggestion (already you know it's not for you) is Yale Hirsch's *Directory of Exceptional Stockbrokers*. ("How much do you have to produce to get in there?" a fledgling stockbroker asked eagerly before I explained that inclusion was not based on production.) Although the 1982 edition is growing a bit stale, it is a manful effort, based on three years' research, to identify 125 solid brokers and to sketch the approaches that have won the approval of their clients and colleagues. The Hirsch Organization (6 Deer Trail, Old Tappan, New Jersey 07675) believes these folks are OK.

But then, so are many mutual funds. The problem with entrusting your funds to either type of stranger is that it robs you of the chance to throw some business your old college roommate's way or to your brother-in-law—not because you really want to do him a favor or because you think he can make you some money, but because it makes you feel good to be able to throw the big bills around like that. (You say I'm projecting? I don't have a brother-in-law and my college roommate went into politics, so how can I be projecting?)

General rule: Brokers are better off not doing business with friends (it can cost them friends) and friends are better off not doing business with brokers (it can cost them money).

The man I want for *my* broker is Olumba Olumba Obu.

"Never in the history of mankind—since the creation of the world, and after the birth and death of our Lord Jesus Christ—has anybody anywhere in the world possessed the tremendous spiritual and supernatural power, universal influence and the over-all authority to determine the fate and the future of people anywhere in the world and at any time, as the Sole Spiritual Head of the Brotherhood of the Cross and Star, Leader *Olumba Olumba Obu.*

"He has the universal power to determine or change the course of events as they affect individuals or institutions. He has the supreme and unquestionable authority to solve all kinds of problems anywhere in the world—whether such problems are of physical, spiritual or material nature."

And he has the wherewithal to take out a full-page ad in the *New York Times* saying all that and a great deal more. "Physically based in Calabar, Nigeria," he was able, for example, to conduct a spiritual X-ray of a Mrs. Grace Cosmos Tom, who at the time of her difficulty was two-and-a-half-years pregnant. By following Olumba Olumba Obu's instructions, the doctors were finally able to deliver Mrs. Tom's baby daughter without incident. (The ad gives no clue as to the weight of the child.)

More to the point—I hope you're paying attention—"the most amazing thing about Leader Olumba Olumba Obu is that the mere mention of His initials, O.O.O., is enough to take anyone out of a grave spiritual, physical or material problem."

You laugh, but there I was short Metromedia, at $212 a share, and there was Metromedia at $560 a share, posing for me a grave material problem. "Oh, oh, oh!" I cried as I looked at Metromedia's price in the paper. *"Oh, oh, oh!"* I wailed. The stock collapsed in short order, saving the day.

10

BOOKS
The Older, the Better

So brokers are out as a surefire source of the financial guidance
you need. How about books? You are, after all, reading one
even now.

Only four great investment books have ever been written,
and I will tell you which they are.

Well, five, maybe, or six, but wait a moment while we get
this into perspective.

It's *tough* to get rich reading books. Tougher still, ironically,
if you choose current ones. Current books are conceived with
great insight. Written at a feverish pace to share that insight,
they are still of some interest when submitted for publication.
Nine months later, when current books first appear, they are
embarrassingly out-of-date. The book on buying strategic metals appears at the height of the strategic-metals boom (so you
should be *selling* metals, not buying them); the book on buying
high-tech stocks appears just as Apple is cresting at 63 (so you
should be *selling* high-tech stocks, not buying them). It's an old
story, retold every season. In mid-1984, it was William Grace's
The Phoenix Approach, a fine new book—but published when
Chrysler, far from being in ashes, had risen tenfold.

People may someday look back on Douglas Casey's *Crisis

Investing, the enormous 1980 best seller that foretold complete economic collapse by 1983, or on Robert Allen's *Creating Wealth,* the enormous 1983 best seller that advised everyone to think positively and buy two rental properties a year, as classics. But for honing one's investment savvy, it may be best to seek out books of statelier vintage.

I was introduced to the *greatest* investment book ever written years ago at business school. I was researching a term paper on chain letters (no less), and my faculty adviser—right off the top of his head—suggested I seek out a volume called *Extraordinary Popular Delusions and the Madness of Krauts,* by Charles Mackay, published, he said, in 1841. My God, I was impressed. What esoterica! (I was also astonished by the title and surprised to learn that Germans, even back in 1841, were called Krauts—or that anyone would have called them that on a book jacket.) I subsequently learned that *any* business professor worth his salt would have had this book at tongue's tip. And that it had to do with the madness of *crowds.*

Should you run off to the library to read it—it is, after all, the greatest money book ever written, never mind that it is 143 years old and not the sort of tome you'd want to underline with a yellow Magic Marker (you may underline either of the two paperback editions presently in print)—you will read of alchemists and crusaders, of witches and geomancers, of animal magnetizers and fortunetellers—forerunners, all, of the modern investment analyst—and you will read about tulips. As you probably know, tulips became the object of such insane and unreasoning desire in seventeenth-century Holland that a single bulb about the size and shape of an onion could fetch a small fortune on any of the several exchanges that had sprung up to trade them. (The author describes one unfortunate Dutch sailor who, having a taste for onions and having been sent down to a rich man's kitchen for breakfast, actually *consumed* one of the priceless bulbs in error.)

As with any true classic, once *Extraordinary Popular Delu-*

sions is read it is hard to imagine *not* having known of it—and there is the compulsion to recommend it to others. Thus did financier Bernard Baruch, who claimed it saved him millions, recommend the book in his charming foreword of 1932. (I was asked to write a foreword to a more recent edition, which is why, to a few readers, these words will sound more than a little familiar.)

"Have you ever seen," Baruch quoted an unnamed contemporary, "in some wood, on a sunny quiet day, a cloud of flying midges—thousands of them—hovering, apparently motionless, in a sunbeam! . . . Yes? . . . Well, did you ever see the whole flight—each mite apparently preserving its distance from all others—suddenly move, say three feet, to one side or the other? Well, *what made them do that?* A breeze? I said a *quiet* day. But try to recall—did you ever see them move directly back again in the same unison? Well, what made them do *that?* Great human mass movements are slower of inception but much more effective."

Suddenly, a few years back, everyone in New York and California was on roller skates. I certainly did not view this as a form of madness, having at the time purchased two pairs myself —nor, at least as of this writing, a "great human mass movement." But all of a sudden, there they were—on roller skates.

Baruch quotes Schiller: " 'Anyone taken as an individual is tolerably sensible and reasonable—as a member of the crowd, he at once becomes a blockhead.' " There are lynch mobs and crusades, runs on banks and fires; in each case, if only people hadn't panicked, they would all have escaped with their lives. There are mass suicides. Eight or ten years ago, there was "the hustle," the object of which was for throngs of people to shift gears on the dance floor in lemminglike unison.

(I have never actually seen a lemming, but I suspect that when I do, I will see more than one.)

The month Baruch wrote his foreword, October 1932, marked the absolute bottom of the stock market crash that had

begun three years earlier. Wild speculation had driven the Dow
Jones industrial average to 381 in October 1929; three years
later, it had fallen to 41. The pendulum invariably swings too
far.

"I have always thought," Baruch reflected, "that if . . .
even in the very presence of dizzily spiraling [stock] prices, we
had all continuously repeated, *'two and two still make four,'*
much of the evil might have been averted. Similarly, even in
the general moment of gloom in which this foreword is written,
when many begin to wonder if declines will ever halt, the appropriate abracadabra may be, *'They always did.'* "

In the late sixties, stock prices again began to spiral dizzily.
Synergy was the new magic word, and what it meant was that
two and two could, under astute management, equal five. It
was alchemy of a sort and enough to drive at least one stock,
in two years, from $6 a share to $140. Not much later, it sold
for $1.

By late 1974, stocks generally had eroded in value to Depression levels. Yet if you'd had the courage in December 1974 to
buck the crowd, gains of 500 and 1,000 percent over the ensuing
three to four years would have been common in your portfolio.

Not that you must be a stock trader to benefit from the perspective *Extraordinary Popular Delusions* provides. Should the
government balance its budget? Should the Fed loosen or
tighten credit? Read a tale of money printing and speculation in
early eighteenth-century France that should give any easy-
money advocate pause. (Read, too, of the hunchback who is
supposed to have profited handily by renting out his hump as a
writing table, so frenzied had the speculation become.) Mackay
describes Frenchmen "ruining themselves with frantic eager-
ness." And then the lunacy spreads to England, where,
Mackay says, "every fool aspired to be a knave."

There have been other good books written about money
since 1841, but only a few hold up. Best known and most likely

to make you money is Benjamin Graham's *The Intelligent Investor* (Harper & Row), first published in 1949 and most recently revised in 1973. It is based on Graham's 1934 textbook, *Security Analysis,* written with David L. Dodd. Relatively few read the latter, or even the former, because the author's conservative precepts require of the reader a willingness to spend long hours of close analysis over a period of years. "Medical men have been notoriously unsuccessful in their security dealings," Graham notes, because "they usually have an ample confidence in their own intelligence and a strong desire to make a good return on their money, without the realization that to do so successfully requires both considerable attention to the matter and something of a professional approach to security values."

Unfortunately, moreover, at least as of this writing, with the Dow above 1100, it's far from easy to find securities that meet Graham's strict tests of value.

There is no magic or hocus-pocus in his approach. It is to buy securities so cheaply, relative to their assets, that over the long run they must almost surely appreciate. It's really not much different from Allen's approach in *Creating Wealth,* only there the field is real estate. Allen would have you sift through scores and scores of properties until you find a seller so "motivated" that he is willing to let his property go for much less than it's worth—or else on extraordinarily favorable terms (which amounts to much the same thing). Neither approach is foolproof, and both take a lot of expertise and time.

For most of us, the market is unbeatable. When it is going up, we may look smart; when it is going down, we may feel dumb. But our ability to predict which way it will go, or which stocks within it will outperform the rest, approximates our ability to predict the weather more than a few days in advance. Burton Malkiel's *A Random Walk Down Wall Street* (W. W. Norton), now eleven years old, is at least a near classic. It explains why you—and the overwhelming majority of professionals—would be better served throwing darts at the stock pages and then standing pat than trying to "beat" the market through the application of any active intelligence or strategy.

And this is largely true. The more actively you flail, the more you lose between the cracks to brokerage commissions and taxes.

Malkiel readily agrees that there are exceptions. A handful of people *can* beat the market with reasonable consistency and by a wide margin. But they're rare.

For most, it's best to see the game for what it largely is—a game—and to approach it with at least a modicum of humor. Toward that end, we have "Adam Smith's" *The Money Game,* fifteen years old and one of the greatest investment books ever written. Like Graham's book, it is well known, so I'll be brief. It is about a time long gone—except for the fact that it may have come back—when everyone buzzed about the market and the corps of eager brokers was swelling like a hernia.

"Smith" was appropriately caustic. Among his more lasting bits of advice: "If you don't know who you are, the stock market is an expensive place to find out."

And: Never fall in love with your stock. "The stock doesn't know you own it." Maybe not, but I can name at least three it would break my heart to sell.

Far less well known and even more delightful is Fred Schwed's *Where Are the Customers' Yachts?* now forty-four years old (available, along with a catalog of scores of lesser curiosities, from Fraser Publishing, Box 494, Burlington, Vermont 05402). The title comes from the story you doubtless know about the out-of-towner on a tour of Manhattan's financial district. "Over there are the bankers' yachts," his tourmaster gestured, "and over there are the brokers' yachts."

"Where are the c-c-c-customers' yachts?" the neophyte is alleged to have stuttered, with unwitting perception.

Schwed quotes "the sinister old gag" that Wall Street is a street with a river at one end and a graveyard at the other.

"This is striking but incomplete. It omits the kindergarten in the middle, and that's what this book is about."

He recalls, too, the old saying about the bulls, the bears and the pigs. The bulls make money and the bears make money—but not the pigs. "It took me some time," says Schwed, "to discover it to be particularly untrue."

Although the game grows ever swifter and more sophisticated, nothing changes that much. ("Experience has shown that usually the bulls are victorious and the bears lose out," wrote Joseph De La Vega in 1688.) There were bright young hustlers then; there are bright young hustlers now. There were brokers pretending to know where the market was going then; there are such brokers now. ("The notion that the financial future is not predictable is just too unpleasant to be given any room at all in the Wall Streeter's consciousness," writes Schwed.) Accounting is as much an art to be made fun of as it ever was. (He tells the story of the old gentleman whose sons and auditors were trying to show him that while business *seemed* to be good, the store was actually losing money. "They were awash in ledgers and statements as they strove to prove their point. Finally the old man spoke. 'Listen,' he said. 'The pushcart that I pushed into this town forty years ago we still have. It is in the storeroom on the sixth floor. Go up and look at it. Check it off. Then everything else you see is profit.' ")

There were margin calls then, there are margin calls now—though fewer of them, since much of the leverage has been regulated out of the game. "If you are a customer receiving margin calls there are a number of things you can do," Schwed writes, "but none of them is good." He recounts the finger-in-the-dike method (sending in more and more money to meet the calls) and the head-in-the-sand method (going off to the Maine woods), but seems to favor the old advice: Never meet a margin call. Let your broker sell out your position and be done with it.

He observes investors as if they were ants running in a variety of directions to accumulate crumbs, unaware of the larger forces at work (an approaching human foot, for example). "Your average Wall Streeter," he says, "faced with nothing profitable to do, does nothing for only a brief time. Then, suddenly and hysterically, he does something which turns out to be extremely unprofitable. He is not a lazy man."

People afraid of ever having any cash Schwed labels "rhinophobes." The term would seem more properly to describe people afraid of their noses; but I do know exactly the sort of people he means. The minute they sell a stock, no matter how overpriced the market, they feel compelled immediately to dump the proceeds back into some *other* stock. God forbid they should ever actually sit with cash.

And he describes another timeless type, "customers of a certain mentality who cannot rid themselves of the idea that the whole business is a contest between broker and customer to see which one gets the other's money." In which regard perhaps you saw the item late last year about the prominent Greene County, Pennsylvania, physician who, apparently a sore loser in this contest, dressed up as Santa Claus, abducted his forty-nine-year-old broker from a Christmas party and tortured him for twelve days.

What's marvelous about Schwed is the devastating simplicity and good humor with which he makes his points. Playing the market, he writes, is like playing poker: " 'Now, boys,' said the hopeful soul, 'if we all play carefully, we can all win a little.' "

With patience and gradual economic progress, that can actually be true of the stock market. We can all win a little. It is *not* a "zero-sum" game. But those two seemingly modest ingredients, patience and economic progress, are anything but assured. Especially the first.

11

ANNUAL REPORTS
Letters from Midas

If there aren't many investment guides that hold up over time, there are even fewer such annual reports. On the one hand, what they tell you is true: about the best way to get an overall picture of a public company is by reading its latest annual report. You'll find out what it does, how it's been doing, and why management is cautiously optimistic about the future. If you're good at ratios and footnotes and financial statements, you may even find out a few things management wasn't eager to highlight. For example, current assets may have held steady at $9 million. But if you look closely, you may see that last year the $9 million was made up of $3 million each in cash, accounts receivable and inventory, while *this* year's $9 million is made up of $6 million in inventory (stuff that hasn't sold), $2.98 million in accounts receivable (stuff that's sold but hasn't been paid for), and $19,000 in cash—which is only marginally more than *you* have in the bank.

Even if you are clever at interpreting this sort of thing, however, I'm not sure reading annual reports will do you any good —at least not with respect to the larger companies that are widely followed on Wall Street—in part because you are competing with some very big money managers who should also be

reasonably clever at interpreting these things, and in part because those big money managers are likely to have gotten most
of this information long before the annual report hit your desk.

What's more, even if from reading an annual report you can
get a pretty good feel for the company, you still have to figure
out whether the stock will go up or down. There's a definite
relationship between the performance of a corporation and the
performance of its stock, but no one's quite figured out what it
is.

Having said all this, there is at least one annual report worth
noting, if only for the contrast it provides to so many others. It
is the annual report of a company called Berkshire Hathaway.

Berkshire Hathaway shareholders have come to expect two
things of their annual report: good news (book value per share
has increased from $19 to $976 in the last nineteen years) and
the unorthodox letter of their chairman, Warren Buffett (who
took over nineteen years ago). Indeed, the chairman's letter
practically *is* the Berkshire Hathaway annual report.

Shareholders get no photographs, no colored inks or foil em-
bossing, no bar charts or graphs—not even a logo. It looks like
the kind of annual you see from a company whose bubble has
finally burst, only Berkshire Hathaway, an insurer with major
holdings in several other industries, is no bubble; and at $1,250
a share, up from $85 seven years ago, it shows no signs of
bursting.

The conventional wisdom in reading annual reports is to
glance at the auditor's opinion, then check the financial results
and the footnotes. The chairman's letter? Save your time. Yet
of such interest are Warren Buffett's letters that they have
drawn a sophisticated following. Requests for reprints even!
The company has assembled a compendium of the past seven
to meet the demand.

"They're wonderful," says Leon Levy of Odyssey Partners,
no minor Wall Street legend himself, whereupon he recounts
the passage that most recently amused him—the one in which

Buffett says he wouldn't have wanted any part of the acquisitions most others were making in 1982. "For in many of these acquisitions," Buffett writes, "managerial intellect wilted in competition with managerial adrenaline. The thrill of the chase blinded pursuers to the consequences of the catch. Pascal's observation seems apt: 'It has struck me that all men's misfortunes spring from the single cause that they are unable to stay quietly in one room.' (Your chairman left the room once too often last year and almost starred in the Acquisition Follies of 1982. In retrospect our major accomplishment of the year was that a very large purchase to which we had firmly committed [fell through] for reasons totally beyond our control. Had it come off, this transaction would have consumed extraordinary amounts of time and energy, all for a most uncertain payoff. If we were to introduce graphics to this report, illustrating favorable business developments of the past year, two blank pages depicting this blown deal would be the appropriate centerfold.)"

"I love that," beams Levy.

Buffett himself says he tries to talk to shareholders as if they were his partners. "I assume I've got a very intelligent partner who has been away for a year and needs to be filled in on all that's happened." He also assumes little turnover among his 2,900 shareholders. "Rather than repeat the same things each year," he says, "I take up topics that further their education." It is an exercise he seems clearly to enjoy—the letters, currently running fourteen printed pages, get longer every year. (The other extreme may have been reached by Wisconsin banker Jack Puelicher, another iconoclastic chief executive, whose letter to Marshall & Ilsley shareholders in the spring of 1983 read, in its entirety: "Your company had a very good year in 1982. Some of it was due to luck; some of it was due to good planning and management. We hope you enjoy the numbers and the pictures.")

Buffett's attention to his letters was sharpened by his service on an SEC panel formed in 1976 to study disclosure practices. (The committee issued a 1,200-page document that concluded the disclosure system was okay.) Former SEC Commissioner A. A. Sommer, Jr., who chaired the committee—himself a Berkshire Hathaway shareholder—says the group felt such letters were very important. Even so, he adds, "Warren's letters are unique. Damn few C.E.O.s are as smart in as many ways as Warren. It would be awfully hard to require that kind of discussion from all C.E.O.s."

Does Buffett ever take on unorthodox subjects in his letters? Yes, he responds, he discusses his mistakes.

"The textile business again had a very poor year," he reported in 1977. (When Buffett first took over Berkshire Hathaway in 1965, that's *all* it was—a New Bedford, Massachusetts, textile manufacturer.) "We have mistakenly predicted better results in each of the last two years. Many difficulties experienced [have been] due primarily to industry conditions, but some of the problems have been of our own making."

"We continue to look for ways to expand our insurance operation," he wrote his shareholders in 1979, "but your reaction to this intent should not be unrestrained joy. Some of our expansion efforts—largely initiated by your chairman—have been lackluster, others have been expensive failures."

Buffett downplays the excellence of his own efforts, but like a proud coach, highlights it in his players. Berkshire Hathaway owns a third of Geico, the auto insurer, and of that company's brass he writes: "Jack Byrne and Bill Snyder are achieving the most elusive of human goals—keeping things simple and remembering what you set out to do."

And of an eighty-one-year-old subsidiary chief, since deceased: "Our experience has been that the manager of an already high-cost operation frequently is uncommonly resourceful in finding new ways to add overhead, while the manager of a tightly run operation usually continues to find additional methods to curtail costs, even when his costs are already well below those of his competitors. No one has demonstrated this latter ability better than Gene Abegg.''

Here and there notes of sentimentality pop up, but if Buffett wants to say something a little silly about the Washington Post Company, for which he delivered papers at the age of thirteen, or Geico, which first caught his eye at twenty, it should be remembered that Berkshire's holdings have appreciated about tenfold in each. So he can say what he likes.

Happily, he says it with a sense of humor. "In a characteristically rash move," he writes, "we have expanded World Headquarters by 252 square feet (17 percent), coincidental with the signing of a new five-year lease." World Headquarters—in Omaha—houses, in addition to Buffett, five other people. ("A compact organization lets all of us spend our time managing the business rather than managing each other.")

Most chairmen's letters describe how well everything went, under the circumstances, hoping the shareholders will buy it. Buffett's stress the negative, knowing that they won't.

In the 1982 report, immediately after observing that Berkshire Hathaway's eighteen-year rise in book value represented a 22 percent compound annual rate of growth, he adds: "You can be certain that this percentage will diminish in the future. Geometric progressions eventually forge their own anchors." (He's right, of course. Maintaining that rate for another eighteen years would mean growing in book value to $22 billion and, after eighteen years more, to nearly $1 million per share.) Geometric progressions eventually forge their own anchors, but in 1983 book value increased yet another 32 percent. (Results for 1984 won't be released until early 1985.) Even when stating that paper gains in the Berkshire Hathaway portfolio were up 40 percent, he is careful first to subtract the taxes that would be paid if those gains were taken.

To be sure, it's easy to be candid and self-deprecatory when any fool can see that you're terrific. What may be a tad galling to some of his peers is that Buffett's letters review not only his own performance and mistakes but those of the rest of the nation's managers as well. "There are indications," he writes, "that several large insurers opted in 1982 for obscure accounting and reserving maneuvers that masked significant deterioration in their underlying businesses. In insurance, as elsewhere, the reaction of weak managements to weak operations is often weak accounting."

His recurring theme: the rights of shareholders, as trampled on by so many other managers.

Well known are the corporate managers who fight heroically to fend off generous tender offers. Less sharply perceived are the managers who pay too much to grow by acquisition. "Managers who want to expand their domain at the expense of owners," Buffett chides wryly, "might better consider a career in government."

It's even worse, in his view, when the acquisition is made with stock, because the acquirer's stock so often sells in the market for a discount to its true value. "The acquirer who nevertheless barges ahead is using an undervalued currency [his stock] to pay for a fully valued property. . . . Friendly investment bankers will reassure him as to the soundness of his actions. (Don't ask the barber whether you need a haircut.)"

In light of the enormous premium required to buy *all* of a company, Buffett's strategy has been one of partial acquisition. Where another company will bid $48 a share for all of a company whose shares were yesterday $25, Buffett is content to buy quietly at $25. "What really makes us dance," he admits, is to buy 100 percent of a business at a good price, but that is awfully hard to do. And so it is that at the start of 1984 Berkshire Hathaway owned, among other things, chunks of Geico (35 percent), General Foods (8.5 percent), precious metals fabricator Handy & Harman (17 percent), R.J. Reynolds (5 percent), Interpublic (6 percent), Ogilvy & Mather (5.5 percent), Time Inc. (1.5 percent), and the Washington Post Company (13 percent).

Berkshire Hathaway's reported earnings include only the dividend income from the companies in its investment portfolio, so Buffett must each year remind shareholders that reported profits exclude a large portion of true earning power. "This is not a criticism of accounting procedures," he hastens to add. "We would not like to have the job of designing a better system. It's simply to say that managers and investors alike must understand that accounting numbers are the beginning, not the end, of business valuation."

Lamenting the complexities of accounting, he reveals that "the Yänomamö Indians employ only three numbers: one, two, and more than two. Maybe their time will come." Meanwhile, in his 1983 letter, he treats shareholders to a quick 2,000-word seminar on the subtleties of accounting for "goodwill" when one company acquires another. (Goodwill, he believes, for all its intangibility, can be a very real asset—often of greater value and durability than plants and equipment. He understands why the $40-million premium over book value one company may pay for another is chalked up to "goodwill"—but notes that the $1 million charge against earnings the acquisitor must take in each of the ensuing 40 years may serve only to understate earnings for 40 years.)

Because of the growing importance of the company's non-consolidated holdings, Buffett argues, it's no longer appropriate for shareholders to gauge Berkshire's performance by the ratio of reported profits to equity, as he used to advise they should. But then he adds: "You should be suspicious of such an assertion. Yardsticks seldom are discarded while yielding favorable readings. But when results deteriorate, most managers favor disposition of the yardstick rather than disposition of the manager. To managers faced with such deterioration, a more flexible measurement system often suggests itself: just shoot the arrow of business performance into a blank canvas and then carefully draw the bull's-eye around the implanted arrow. We generally believe in pre-set, long-lived, and small bull's-eyes."

One of the bull's-eyes he considers notably unimpressive is the widely trumpeted achievement of "record earnings." "After all," he explains, "even a totally dormant savings account will produce steadily rising interest earnings each year because of compounding."

It's no surprise that Buffett would champion shareholders' rights; at fifty-two, he has long been a professional shareholder himself. He and his wife own shares in Berkshire Hathaway that were recently worth $600 million, and Berkshire Hathaway is itself largely in the business of owning shares.

Author "Adam Smith" (Jerry Goodman), in *Supermoney*, labels Buffett "easily the outstanding money manager of the generation," noting that a partnership he began in 1956—and had the consummate foresight to close down in 1969—achieved a compound annual growth of 31 percent. "What was more remarkable," writes Goodman, "was that he did it with the philosophy of another generation . . . just pure Benjamin Graham, applied with absolute consistency." I told you Graham's book could make you money! Buffett chose Graham as a mentor (and years later, Graham chose Buffett to help revise his book).

Although Graham and Buffett did not agree on all things, their common perception was to buy assets so cheaply that over time they could hardly fail to profit. This approach, as noted in the previous chapter, calls for a level head and hard work. "The market, like the Lord," Buffett writes, "helps those who help themselves. But, unlike the Lord, the market does not forgive those who know not what they do."

Buffett's strategy of partial acquisition makes sense when companies are selling in the marketplace at a substantial discount to their true value as ongoing businesses, but not when the market, as it periodically does, jumps over the moon. In 1972, with Avon and some of the other glamour stocks selling at sixty times earnings, Berkshire had only 15 percent of its portfolio in equities, vs. 80 percent at the end of 1982. "There were as many good businesses around in 1972 as in 1982," he writes, "but the prices the stock market placed upon those businesses in 1972 looked absurd." Should the stock market keep climbing, he warned in early 1983, Berkshire's "ability to utilize capital effectively in partial-ownership positions will be reduced or eliminated. We currently are seeing early traces of this problem." (Damn—another bull market.)

Among the final notes in most of Buffett's letters is a virtual BUSINESSES WANTED classified. It tells a lot about how Warren Buffett operates. Berkshire Hathaway, Buffett writes, is look-ing for large, simple businesses ("if there's lots of technology, we won't understand it") with consistent earning power, little debt, management in place ("we can't supply it"), and an offer-ing price ("we don't want to waste our time or that of the seller by talking, even preliminarily, when price is unknown.") "We will not engage in unfriendly transactions. We can promise complete confidentiality and a very fast answer as to possible interest—customarily within five minutes."

Happily, one company did fit the bill in 1983. Was it Martin Marietta or Disney? Was it Getty Oil or TWA? No, it was Rose Blumkin's furniture store. Recalling Pascal's line from the pre-vious year's letter about men's misfortunes springing from their inability to stay quietly in one room, Buffett writes, "Even Pascal would have left the room for Mrs. Blumkin."

Rose Blumkin, ninety, founded the Nebraska Furniture Mart in 1937. Under her management it has grown into a single 200,000 square-foot Omaha store that does $100 million a year. So good are the prices she offers, competitors used to sue to shut her down. In one such instance, Buffett reports, Mrs. Blumkin not only won the case in court, she sold the judge $1,400 worth of carpet. In 1983, Berkshire Hathaway bought 90 percent of Nebraska Furniture Mart, leaving 10 percent of the stock for Rose Blumkin's son, Louie, and other key family-member managers.

Given his track record, one is tempted to invest all one's

money in Berkshire Hathaway and let Warren Buffett worry about making it grow, but then one would be forgetting the Second (diversify) and Fourth (you are buying a stock, not a company) Basic Rules of Personal Finance (after all, Berkshire's price might already reflect Buffett's unique abilities), not to mention the Fifth (beware the permanent trend—he could stumble) and the First (buy low, sell high).

Nothing comes easy.

There remain two other avenues of possible financial enlightenment: the business press and your daily mail.

12

THE PRESS

A Plan to Enrich
Financial Reporters
(and, Thereby, the News)

Victor Palmieri, business fix-it superstar, who at the time was in the process of salvaging Penn Central and who may now spend the rest of his life trying to salvage Baldwin-United, strode into our Harvard Business School classroom and dove in.

"What is the first thing you do when you go in to rescue a failing company?" he asked.

"Fire people?" volunteered one of my confrères.

"No. Yes?" Palmieri asked another upraised hand.

"Assure key people that they won't be fired."

"No. What's the *first thing* you do?"

"Negotiate extended credit with your suppliers."

"No. Yes?"

"Make a plan."

"No. The *first* thing. Yes?"

"Make a strong show of command."

"No. Yes?"

This went on past the point of being challenging, past the

point of being amusing, past the point of being embarrassing. Finally, Palmieri gave his answer.

"Nail down the cash!" Meaning, make sure no money can leave the company without your signature.

It was, admittedly, a sensible first thing to do. How could seventy-five brilliant young business students fail to think of it? Perhaps it was that we had had no firsthand experience in such a situation.

With that in mind, consider a highly paid financial reporter I know who takes pride in the fact that he owns no stock. Never has. Well, thirteen shares of A.T.&T. for his daughter, he says, to be entirely forthright and to get a laugh. Fair enough. The guy does great reporting, works like a demon, has high standards (but is less than prescient in his market predictions).

The presumption is: a financial writer should not own stocks. Conflict of interest, otherwise. And, of course, it is true that a financial writer must never own stocks he writes up favorably, nor short one he plans to knock. (Nor—lest we forget David Winans at the *Wall Street Journal*—let others know what's coming.)

But is the reporter who only pays utility bills, say, more objective in writing about utility rate requests than the reporter who owns some stock in one as well? And forgetting objectivity, what about savvy? Could it be that playing the game helps to understand it?

I raise all this not to try to goad my colleague into buying more A.T.&T. (thirteen shares?), but rather as a possible explanation for the less than totally realistic view we financial reporters sometimes have, and paint. Take, for example, the way the press handled October 1979's stock market "crash" ("The Great Crash of '79," the *New York Times* called it), an event by now long forgotten—unless you happen to have lost ten or a hundred thousand dollars in it—but instructive nonetheless.

On Saturday evening of that Columbus Day weekend, Paul Volcker announced a full 1 percent hike in the discount rate.

Ordinarily, these hikes had been coming a quarter of a point at a time, if that. Monday, although a bank holiday, saw the stock market decline sharply. Tuesday, on very heavy volume, the Dow fell more than 26 points. Wednesday, with summer gone just three weeks, it snowed up and down the East Coast—and the market traded a then unbelievable 81.6 million shares, one-third more than any previous day in history. The market fell enough by noon to suggest events were truly coming unhinged, but recovered much of the day's loss by the close. Wednesday's "frenzy" would be attributed by the *Times* and others, accurately, to "panic selling by small investors." What made them panic? Could it have had anything to do with the news media?

The stories I read and saw on television in the heat of the moment all said much the same thing: "Wall Street was spooked by fears of a much sharper than expected recession"; Wall Street was spooked by the impending fiftieth anniversary of the October 29, 1929, market crash (which the press had been highlighting relentlessly in "nostalgia features" the weeks before); Wall Street, obviously, was not happy with Volcker's move and apparently thought it would fail. (Why else would investors be unloading their stocks?)

Ordinarily, of course, the little one-line explanations that sum up the day's stock market activity on the evening news are not just lightweight—they don't matter. The Dow drops three-and-a-half points, which is to say very little indeed, and, instead of reporting that "nothing much happened on Wall Street today," the news naturally goes for something a little better. "The Dow dropped *more than* three points," will go the report (or "nearly four points"—but never *"less than"* four points or *"barely"* three points). "Analysts attributed the decline to nervousness over anticipated money supply figures." Hogwash, perhaps, but no harm done.

It is another matter how these things are reported when the market is falling precipitously and when there's a touch of hysteria in the air. Then something *is* happening, and it *is* worth trying to report the cause accurately. Because if there is a clear, logical cause it is less likely to be "scary" and to touch off unreasoning selling.

Almost none of the news reports in those first two or three nervous days—perhaps because many of the reporters and their editors themselves were not investors—provided a clear, logical explanation.

Why did the market plunge?

For every $100 I had in the market as Paul Volcker was speeding home with instructions from foreign central bankers to take drastic action or else, about $15 was borrowed from my broker. This seemed pretty smart to me at the time. Even now I can think of dumber things I have done in my lifetime—although none springs to mind right away. Nonetheless, Volcker announced his money-tightening measures and there was suddenly the prospect of having to pay 16½ percent interest on my borrowed funds, maybe more. (As it turned out, more.) I thought about that briefly and decided that, good as were the values in the stock market, 16½ percent was more interest than I would enjoy paying. And it was evident that others would feel the same way. And that still others, who had no margin loans outstanding themselves, but who would expect those who did to sell, would want to sell, too.

When interest rates rise gradually, people tend to come to these decisions over a period of time—and the market declines gradually. But when the rate jumps a full point and world attention is focused on it—over a weekend, no less, so there is a full Sunday to contemplate the effects—you can expect a lot of people to get the same idea by Monday morning. In fact, Monday's drop of only 13.87 in the Dow was really much worse in the non-Dow stocks—the type that are more likely to be bought on margin.

Monday night's media coverage, and then Tuesday's, mentioned precious little by way of rational explanation, stressing, instead, vague fears of deep recession, and making nervous allusions to 1929—so that even though the market would most likely have dropped Tuesday and Wednesday anyway, it perhaps dropped a good bit more than it otherwise would have.

The basic media interpretation: while many business leaders and bankers were favorably disposed to the Fed's strong medicine, Wall Street apparently was not.

Nothing could have been more misleading. Wall Street was *pleased* with Volcker's action. And yet investors (and speculators) sold. Why? Because they didn't want to borrow at these rates, or knew others wouldn't want to.

Which, indeed, was the whole point of the Volcker move. To brake the growth in the money supply. To get people to pay off loans, rather than borrow more. To shock rather than move gradually, in order to demonstrate the seriousness with which the Fed would fight inflation. To precipitate recession in order to prevent something even worse. So Wall Street did applaud the move, even while it sold stocks; and the press got it all backward.

The following Monday, *New York* magazine's Jack Egan would be quoting a Wall Street pro: "Everyone who is short-term oriented is running to exit from the stock market; everyone who is long-term oriented is very bullish on the future. But they're not exactly rushing in to buy yet." Such a quote (or *Business Week*'s sensible coverage, and that of others) would have come in handy on "Eyewitness News" in the heat of the moment. Instead, for example, you had as the *New York Times* "quotation of the day" on Thursday morning: "People are in a state of confusion. People are scared by the moves by the Federal Reserve this weekend, and no one knows what's going to happen next." Pretty scary, no? A better quotation might have been: "It kills me to sell stocks when they're this cheap, but I'm not going to borrow at these crazy rates. I've sold enough to pay off my margin debts."

Clearly, what's needed is to give all financial reporters and

editors, headline writers and quotation choosers, $250,000 each
in stocks, bonds, and futures contracts. Get us all into the
game. The caliber of financial reporting would pick right up.

In the meantime—as if you didn't know it—you should not
pay *too* much attention to the instant financial analyses you
read or, for that matter—read on—hear on radio or TV.

ALL THE NEWS THAT'S FIT FOR PRINT

The President of the United States had just been shot, and Bill
Rukeyser, "Good Morning America's" regular guest for this
kind of thing, was on vacation. (Bill Rukeyser is editor of *Fortune*.) The call came to me: would I come on GMA to tell David
Hartman and the world why the stock market went down when
the President of the United States was shot? And why it went
back up when it appeared he would recover? A limousine was
sent to drive me the half-mile from my home to the studio. I
explained that the stock market had gone down when the President was shot because this was perceived as bad news; and
that it had gone back up again because word that he'd recover
was reassuring. For this I was paid $250.

Not that you'd want to risk hiring some piker to interpret
events—save a few bucks, but risk getting it wrong. ("The
market plunged on fears of lower first-quarter profits.")

Financial and economic matters, once relegated to the print
media, and relegated even there to one crusty old fellow with a
desk and a ticker someplace way off in the back of the news-
room, have captured national attention—ever since the national pie stopped growing and people became increasingly
concerned, understandably, over the size of their slice.

Where once television programmers would doubtless have
preferred dead air to business news—at least with dead air
some people might stay tuned to see what would come on next
—today it is becoming difficult to flip a television dial, particu-

larly if it's hooked to a cable box, without running through two
or three such reports. And more are on the way. They range
from ninety-second business reports beamed around the country, to the weekly half-hour "Wall Street Journal Report."

Clearly, the quality of TV business coverage has improved
and will continue to do so. But there are still lots of on-camera
people, particularly at the local level, who read the business
news with no clue as to what it means (which, for one thing, is
why they often confuse "millions" and "billions"). This can
hardly be said of ABC's Dan Cordtz (formerly of *Fortune,* before that with the *Wall Street Journal*); CBS's Ray Brady (former editor and columnist of *Dun's Review,* before that with
Forbes); or NBC's Mike Jensen (former *New York Times* financial reporter, before that business and financial editor of the
Boston *Herald Traveler*)—to name just three. But although the
networks hit the headlines pretty well, they do not begin to
provide the depth available in print.

It's an old story that TV news provides less depth than print
journalism, but it goes beyond that. The *proportion* of traditional TV news devoted to business and economics is smaller
than it is on the front pages of most decent daily newspapers.

The problem is, business isn't terribly well suited to television. It's often dull. It's complex. It's not visual. Programmers
know this, but they also know it's important, and they're mind-
ful of the advertising rates upscale audiences command. And
so you have Louis Rukeyser, whose "Wall Street Week" on
PBS is the granddaddy of this whole thing (and who is Bill
Rukeyser's brother), branching off with a show, since canceled,
called Louis Rukeyser's "Business Journal." "Business Journal" had fascinating segments on the business of a rock group,
on the business of the Super Bowl, on the business of selling
Girl Scout cookies—anything, in short, but the business of
business. ("Well, if we actually did the show about business,"
you can just hear the producers saying, "nobody would watch
it!")

And so, too, you've had Howard Ruff, "America's most out-spoken and outrageous financial adviser," taping a syndicated hour-long financial series, "Ruff Company," that featured, in one of the shows, a half-hour interview with radio sex coun-selor Dr. Ruth Westheimer. Ruff believes Dr. Westheimer is exploiting sex as a way of attracting a listenership. Only for that reason, he says, and because he believes morality and eco-nomics are intertwined, did he lead off *his* hour with provoca-tive snippets from her show.

"Wall Street Week" succeeds without sex because its targets are the few million Americans who follow the market. This is their *money* we are talking about—there are few subjects more compelling—even if, in fact, as seems likely, they will not make any more of it by watching "Wall Street Week." These folks enjoy securities talk as others enjoy sports talk. Rukeyser makes it good clean fun. But how do you make business and finance interesting to the other 95 percent of America?

And beyond a certain point, why does television have to? Anyone who needs to know more than is reported on the news need only subscribe to the *Wall Street Journal.* By and large, business news and analysis are better suited to print than tele-vision. The obvious advantages: the reader can flip past stories and ads that don't interest him while pondering the paragraphs and pie charts that do.

This isn't to say I don't sit mesmerized from time to time watching the Financial News Network, with its stock ticker running continuously across the bottom of the screen and a woman named Liebe Geft, who elicits more viewer mail than any other feature of the twelve-hour-a-day programming, read-ing and analyzing movement in the futures markets. The FNN crew does a good job—but who has time for this?

Another fine effort for which you may not have time is "The Nightly Business Report," originating from Miami. On what was then the second busiest day in the history of the New York Stock Exchange, "The Nightly Business Report" aborted its usual news coverage to air a thirty-minute special on annual meetings. Yet, despite the unfortunate scheduling (the result, as it turned out, of a satellite malfunction), this is where TV can shine: in showing us the actual people, the actual things. There was corporate gadfly Evelyn Y. Davis, whom many of us have read about but few of us have "met," gushing on about how "important" and "glamorous" she is. There, also, a chief executive being brutally assailed by an angry stockholder.

But if angry shareholders make for good television, corporate executives generally do not. Out of the glare of the lights and camera, executives will provide colorful, pointed interviews— especially if assured certain quotes won't be attributed. On camera, they are inhibited and dull. In a printed story, three days of reporting and interviewing can be distilled into a brisk, polished read. Contrast that with, say, having to listen to a business-school dean talking for thirty undistilled minutes on CNN's "Inside Business" segment on the general direction of graduate business education. You could read the essence of what he had to say in a minute and a half. Tops.

And then there are the shows on "personal finance." Morning exercise may be easier with the help of TV; the way to a successful soufflé may be clearest through the eye of an overhead camera. But personal finance, unlike bending or blending, can be handled more effectively in print.

Nor is there much ability, in some TV situations, for fact-checking or "editing." And so it is that you have Venita VanCaspel ("The Moneymakers") smiling and nodding as her guest says $150,000 at 10 percent will compound to $600,000 by 1987. What is Venita to do? The man said it, she was nodding. Even if the error is caught before the tape is duplicated for syndication, they can't very well dub in the correct figure— $240,000—or flash a subtitle: THE INFORMATION YOU HAVE JUST HEARD IS WRONG.

This is not to say, of course, that print journalists never err, or that the expanding portfolio of money and economics programs on TV are not, for the most part, highly competent. There have been, moreover, some outstanding special series, such as John Kenneth Galbraith's thirteen-part "Age of Uncertainty"; Milton Friedman's ten-part "Freedom to Choose"; and the WGBH series "Enterprise."

Ironically, much of the best business stuff on TV has come from programs not dedicated to business—a Felix Rohatyn interview on CBS Cable's now defunct "Signature"; *Barron's* editor Alan Abelson every morning for two minutes on "NBC News at Sunrise"; CNN's "Crossfire" grilling David Stockman; "CBS Reports" on the shameful machinations of the tobacco industry; "Sixty Minutes" on the sale of overpriced insurance to the poor.

It's not that I wish the more specialized financial programs ill —far from it. The information they provide is accurate, their people come off far more effectively and professionally on TV than I ever have. They just don't talk as fast as I can read.

13

JUNK MAIL
Free! 100 Shares of Stock in a Public Company

Seven hundred million *trillion* tons of junk mail are sent out across this country every year. I get half of it.

Much of it would make me rich if only I would listen. "More explosive price action ahead in low-priced stocks," reads one envelope. "No-risk triple bonus offer enclosed!"

"Inside," reads another, "find out how $8,750 grew to $405,125 in only 13 weeks!"

"Free!" reads a third, "Get 100 Shares of Stock in a Public Company with This No-Risk Offer."

A hundred shares of stock free? Wow! I wonder which stock it is. General Foods? Hewlett Packard? Sears? The letter doesn't say.

The way to deal with junk mail is not even to look at it. Anything that arrives with less than twenty cents postage or a computer-generated address label gets tossed out unopened.

Which is why advertising copywriters have begun reserving their most inspired moments not for the messages printed inside the envelopes but for the messages outside. Somehow, between the time you bend your right wrist, clawlike, to clasp the top envelope in the pile cradled in your left hand and the time, a moment later, you flick that same wrist to send the envelope flying for the trash—somehow in that moment a message of such urgency and intrigue must be conveyed as to stun you in midflick.

Examples abound.

From Mutual of Omaha: "If You Think *$2.00* Doesn't Buy Much Anymore, Look Inside . . . *You'll Be Amazed!*" ("Oh, my God, Meg, come and look at this! They're selling *insurance!*") Who would'a thunk it.

From *Mother Jones*: "URGENT REMINDER ENCLOSED." (The deadline for Christmas gift subscriptions was fast approaching.)

From an address in Washington: "Ted Kennedy hopes you'll throw this away!!" (Out it goes.)

Bulk-rate from "The Honorable Ronald Wilson Reagan, President of the United States." (Oh, that Ronald Wilson Reagan.) Wonder what he could want. Out it goes.

From the American Civil Liberties Union: "An Open Letter to President Reagan." (Gosh! Letters *to* Reagan, *from* Reagan . . . Should I forward it?) Out it goes.

From *International Living*: "You can now earn up to $80,000 TAX-FREE by living abroad . . ." (assuming you have the skills to earn $80,000 and don't mind living abroad).

Some junk mail can be strangely personal—and not just because of the strange ways they stick your name, or variants thereon, into the advertising copy.

From a doctor in San Antonio: "Are you over 40? [No.] You could be missing out on the best sex of your entire life! [Really?] To find out why, see inside. [Well, it can't hurt to look.]"

From *Ovation* magazine, bulk rate, a "special invitation" from my cousin Andre Previn. As it is the first and only communication I have ever had from my spectacularly gifted cousin, verbal, visual or otherwise—I've never met him—and as my middle name is Previn (really—we're cousins), I am sorely tempted to open it. Out it goes.

From a company in Illinois: "Do you have a system for getting organized that works?" They have a wall-sized calendar.

A hazard in throwing all this out unopened is that you won't know what you're missing. Take the envelope headlined: "Me? Sleep in a subway station?" Either some wonderfully creative real estate developer had hit upon renovating unused subway stations (in which case I was being offered a "great space, no view"), or this was an appeal to aid New York's homeless. We'll never know. And what are we to make of: "Demand a nuclear-free New York!" Was New York planning to join the arms race? Or was this about the Shoreham, Long Island, nuclear power plant? You'd assume the latter, but judging from the fine print—still on the outside of the envelope—you'd be wrong. It was about the stationing of missiles someplace upstate, when, of course, everyone knows they should all be stationed up in Somebody Else's state.

Junk mail can depress you—what can you expect from an envelope marked "Urgent" and sent from the World Mercy Fund?—but there's actually quite a lot of celebrating going on. The amazing Mutual of Omaha offer referenced above was in celebration of Mutual's seventy-fifth anniversary. The Visiting Nurse Service of New York was recently looking for $90 donations in celebration of its ninetieth anniversary. A company selling quartz watches for just $2 ("this is not a misprint") was doing so—all this explained on the outside of the envelope— "to celebrate the 10 millionth watch sale of the famous New York jewelry firm of Abernathy & Closther." Surely you know the firm.

I love the ones marked, *Personal and Confidential* down by my name, and *Blk Rt* in the upper right. And, of course, I get a lot of animal mail. It is very hard to resist.

"Inside: an urgent appeal to stop the killing of 6,000,000 animals . . . Open At Once."

Six million animals? How endangered could they be if there

are six million of them? What are we talking here—hogs? chickens? Oh, God . . . okay, I'll open it.

The appeal proved to be from the Kangaroo Protection Foundation. One might think this largely an Australian issue, but apparently it's all our fault for lifting the ban on kangaroo skin importation. We did so, according to the letter, "under intense pressure from the Australian government," which, democratically elected though it may have been, obviously knows nothing about the wishes of the Australian people, who are, the letter says, all batshit over the kangaroo harvest.

The compromise I worked out with the KPF—having opened these letters, one must rationalize one's nonresponse—was this: I would send no money, but neither would I ever eat or wear anything even remotely marsupial.

Why should I? I have more than enough other delicacies available parcel post.

From the Collin Street Bakery: "What Bordeaux is to wine and Maine is to lobster, Corsicana, Texas, is to fruitcake—the New York *Times*." The bakery's so darn proud of that fruitcake, a four-color mouthful of it peeks out at you through a Texas-shaped plasticene window. These are, furthermore, *guaranteed* fruitcakes (I couldn't resist: I opened the envelope). If you or your friends have *ever* tasted better, your money is refunded. Bob McNutt, Bill McNutt and Bill McNutt III stand behind that promise, and Gene Autry and the Kuwait Oil Company are among the list of Distinguished Clientele. We're talking serious fruitcake here.

And from Cheeselovers International (never mind how I get on these lists): "If you find a 3-inch PINK SLIP in this envelope, you have won a diamond necklace in our $1,000.00 Sweepstakes."

I don't wear jewelry, but that is only because I've been waiting to win a Cheeselovers International diamond necklace. I opened the envelope.

The letter begins: "Dear Cheeselover, Before you look at a

single cheese—search through this envelope. If you find a 3-inch colored slip it may be your lucky day. And if the colored slip you find is *pink* it means you have won a genuine diamond solitaire necklace. To claim your prize, just follow the directions on the pink slip. [The cheesewriter seems awfully confident that I'll find a pink slip.] Then—once you've calmed down (if you are a winner)—look at our delicious cheeses.'' (Special this month: the Creme de Menthe Cheese Ball, "the most sophisticated cheese spread of all.'' Move over, Velveeta!)

Well, it did take me a while to calm down, let me tell you. Because naturally, like everyone else who got this mailing, I found a pink slip. But I never bothered to claim my free necklace (which cost $2 for shipping), because I had a feeling the diamond might be kind of smaller than the one I'd been dreaming of.

Actually, I was lucky to be offered a diamond necklace of any size. (Hey, fella, what more do you want?) My August Cheeselovers letter had declared prominently across the outside of the envelope: NOTICE OF REMOVAL. I risked being struck from their mailing list if I didn't order some cheese. The next month I got an envelope that said: "GOODBYE. This may be the last letter you receive from us.'' And now, a month later still, and still having ordered no cheese, they were giving me a diamond necklace.

I'm being unkind. Cheeselovers creme de menthe cheese balls are probably just fine, and for a certain segment of America, Cheeselovers must really pep up the morning's mail. The segment I have in mind would include Calvin Klein's girl in the trailer in rural Georgia—you know, the one who has these friends? Dot and Earl? Who have this dream? They have this dream that one day, *one day*—they dream that *one day!* they'll see Atlanta!

The diamond, I discovered someplace in the mailing, was a 17-facet quarter-point stone. Say, hey, Jose! A little calculation (there are 100 points in a carat, a carat is a fifth of a gram, a gram is 3.5 hundredths of an ounce) produced a gem weighing nearly 18 millionths of an ounce. Diamond dust.

But if diamonds are not a great investment, and if getting them free for $2 apiece from Cheeselovers International is not the best means of acquisition, there's no lack of mail to tell you what is.

Here's an envelope that promises to tell "How you could have made 1,555 percent—*without* being an investment expert!" Of course, the implication that investment experts make 1,555 percent is almost as absurd as that by opening this envelope and signing up for this service, you will, too.

The headline on the back reads: "How a $10,000 investment became more than $165,000 since 1975!" A footnote beneath the text next to the chart on the back of the envelope confesses that this was a "hypothetical" $10,000. But it *would'a* grown to $165,000 if only this service had discovered and promoted its magic formula back in 1975. There follows the SEC inspired disclosure that "Past results are not necessarily a guarantee for equivalent future results"—the understatement of the age— particularly since, in this case, the "past results" were hypothetical.

(You tell me what happened over the last ten or twenty years, and I'll construct a sure-fire strategy that would have worked magnificently if only you had followed it. One such involves buying stocks whenever a premerger NFL football team wins the Super Bowl, and shorting them whenever an AFL team wins. As Professor Steven Goldberg has pointed out, far more remarkable than this coincidental correlation would have been someone's *predicting* it. No one did.)

For $96 a year you get to see whether a strategy that would have worked over the past eight years is the right one for the next eight. What's more, there's "No emotional involvement. No guesswork. No worry." Just follow the monthly advice. Like connect-the-dots, only at the end you're rich. What's more, if after two months you're not pleased with the newsletter (how can you assess its performance after two months?), you can get your money back—less the $16 you paid for the first two issues and any money you may have lost following its advice.

Or perhaps you'd rather "Profit by Learning Politicians' Dirty Little Secrets," as another envelope invited . . . "a Unique New Publication for the Sophisticated Investor," just $275 a year. Isn't that great? Here you have scores of sophisticated reporters for *The Economist* and the *Wall Street Journal* struggling to come up with the occasional secret, and these two guys (two guys write it) come up with a newsletter full of dirty little secrets month after month after month.

But why spend good money to get rich—hey, a dollar's a dollar—when the very next envelope in the pile promises a *free* report on HOW TO ACHIEVE FINANCIAL INDEPENDENCE IN THE NEXT THREE YEARS? I *ache* to open the envelope. Pressing real tight, I can even see the words IRON-CLAD GUARANTEE showing through from the inside. But you know my rule about junk mail. Out it goes.

Because really, if you sift long enough, you will eventually come upon an envelope that will not only make you rich, like the others, and at no cost to you, like the one above, but *without your even having to open it.* Like this one bulk mailed from Howard Lake, Minnesota, emblazoned: "The Dow will pass 2300 . . . Silver will hit $95/oz . . . The prime rate will sink to 8 percent . . . Housing values will gain 30-50 percent . . . all within 18 months!" The envelope goes on to promise "10 more profitable forecasts for 1984–85 from the fastest-growing investment analysis service in America," but the four on the outside of the envelope more than suffice. Just sell everything else and buy silver.

Too easy? Nothing worthwhile comes free? Okay, go ahead and pay the subscription fee ($150, *The Money Advocate*).

The rub comes when one of your $150 newsletters is saying

one thing and another, the other. (Or when both are saying the same thing and both prove wrong.) This happens all the time.

Who's right? you wonder—and, as if by telepathy, comes, bulk rate, a buff and maroon envelope headlined just that way. "Who's right?" It enumerates contrasting predictions by Howard Ruff and Harry Browne (gold will zoom; no it won't); Vern Myers and James Blanchard (deflation is unstoppable; 30 to 35 percent inflation's around the corner); the Aden Sisters and Mark Skousen (gold's going to $4,000; don't hold your breath). *Gee!* All these preeminent experts, strangely full of praise for each other and frequently touting each other's pricey monthly poop sheets—"Who's right?"

"At last, you can find out! (see inside)."

One examines the envelope in hope of unmasking this arbiter of investment prediction, this forecaster's forecaster, this Edgar Cayce of international finance, but there's no return address. So we'll never know who it is unless we open the envelope, and you know the rule. *

Junk costs 11 cents to mail if it's under 3.9111 ounces, or 5.2 cents if under 3.5708 ounces and the sender's nonprofit. Heavier pieces are lumped together and charged by the pound: 45 cents commercial, 23.3 cents nonprofit. But if you bundle by zip code you knock off nine-tenths of a cent if you're nonprofit, 1.7 cents if you're not—are you writing all this down?—and if you sort by carrier route, as well, subtract yet another penny (nonprofit) or 1.9 cents (commercial). You can tell the Vita-Mix Corporation sorts its urgent bulk mail by zip and carrier route

---

* One set of envelopes I do consistently open comes from American Express's Travel Related Services Company. I open them to see just how far the concept "travel-related" can be stretched. No fewer than three such travel-related offers came in one day's mail not long ago. One was for a $540 Vidal Sassoon Infinity Necklace (sorry, I get all my jewelry from Cheeselovers); another offered goblets engraved with my name and crest; the third offered a dozen crystal paperweights, presumably to keep my papers from flying all over while I'm off traveling.

("Please Rush. Dated Material Enclosed.") by the thrifty 7.4 cents metered on each envelope.

Swamped by all this stuff? "Too bad, Tobias," reads the caption of a cartoon showing through the window of an envelope designed to catch me in midflick—"I *told* you reading 43 newspapers would warp your mind!" This would appear to be the beginning of a pitch for a news digest newsletter, not to be confused with a newsletter digest newsletter, several of which solicit with equal enthusiasm. The style of the cartoon is suspiciously like one that shows through the window of another envelope, in which I am apparently in the midst of a tax audit. "Tobias," says the auditor, "you should be *proud* to be a tax-paying American." "I am! I am!" I apparently say, but a little balloon above my head shows I am thinking I could be just as proud on half the taxes.

Personalized junk mail cartoons! I'll bet they don't have them in Russia. Does this mean ten years from now we'll be watching cable TV and the cable box atop our set will insert our names into the audio whenever the commercial broadcaster leaves a coded blank? ("You deserve a break today—Tobias—at McDonald's.") And will that spell the end of junk mail as we know it?*

These are heavier questions than I mean to ask or dare to answer. The question I should address—no snap either—is whether any of these financial newsletters can make you money.

Some undoubtedly can. But which?

"Would you pay $5 per month to find out whose investment advice really works?" asks an envelope. To which the sensible

---

* If you really want to stem the tide of junk mail, they claim all you have to do is write the Direct Mail Advertising Association to get your name on a list to be taken off the other lists. I've never done this, in part because I can't believe it would work, and in part because on some level I must enjoy getting all this mail. Like the shaver who complains about shaving but would never want bald cheeks.

reply is, "No, but I'd pay $5,000 a month to know whose *will*." For there's the problem. It's easy to find newsletters (or mutual funds or brokers or crapshooters) who've had a great couple of years; not at all easy to judge which will.

The concept of a $135-a-year newsletter called the *Hulbert Financial Digest* (409 First Street S.E., Washington, D.C. 20003), which tracks the performance of a variety of other newsletters, is to find the ones with the hot hands and climb on board while they're hot; then deftly abandon ship (before everybody else does) when their hands begin to cool. Never mind that most of your gains, if you have gains, will likely be short-term and thus heavily taxed. It's particularly important to bail out ahead of everyone else when a letter has developed a following. When 5,000 of you go to sell 300 shares apiece of some $13 stock—well, 1.5 million shares may be more than the market can absorb in one day without the price slipping a point or four. (Indeed, the hot hands get hotter, at least for a while, because their recommendations are frequently, in the short run, self-fulfilling.)

One of the hottest hands over the past five years has belonged to Dr. Martin Zweig, whose $245 *Zweig Forecast* (747 Third Avenue, New York, N.Y. 10017) is published every three weeks, with special bulletins when conditions warrant and a hotline you can call for daily comment. Marty Zweig is a smart and personable fellow. Whether paying him $245 a year will greatly improve your lot in life I cannot say. On the back page of each newsletter, there's a listing of his open positions (the things he's recommended you buy), along with the paper profit or loss you would have made on each one. At the bottom of the list is a figure for average profit: 12.9 percent in the most recent letter, although I don't believe it takes into account brokerage commissions or taxes.

This figure doesn't attempt to include all the wonderful profits you may have reaped from Dr. Zweig's past recommendations—only the profit or loss on the position he suggests you still hold. It's not a weighted average in any way—just the sum of sixteen profit and loss percentages divided by sixteen. What's interesting to me is the temptation Dr. Zweig must be under not to recommend sale of the first two entries on his list, IBM, up 66 percent from where he recommended it in July 1982, and Walgreen, up 98.5 percent. In fact, a footnote shows he sold *half* these positions at significantly lower prices . . . but has not yet had the heart to recommend sale of the other half. In part this may be because he thought IBM, even when it hit 130, was still cheap (he had sold the first half at 83), and in part —if he's human—it may be because he hated to see that winner removed from the top of his list in every subsequent issue of the newsletter. Likewise Walgreen, which he had bought at 17. Half he sold at 25, but the other half he recommended holding even when it hit 40. Was it really, at 40, one of the sixteen best buys he could find for his subscribers—or would it simply have been a shame to have to drop it from his list? Without those two magnificent holdovers, IBM and Walgreen, the average gain before commissions and taxes on the other fourteen open positions in the issue of the newsletter I'm looking at would have been 3 percent.

It's got to be a nightmare to have tens of thousands of people scrutinizing every investment decision you make, so I sympathize with Dr. Zweig if he held onto IBM and Walgreen to keep the back page of his newsletter looking good (and I have no proof that he did). The nightmare is in part ameliorated by the $245 a year each of those tens of thousands of onlookers tosses into the pot, but let's not begrudge *The Zweig Forecast* that money. In 1981 and 1982 followers of Zweig's recommendations would have gotten it back in spades and shovels and wheelbarrows. Zweig was great. In 1983 and at least the early part of 1984, they could have done about as well as Zweig in a Sealy Posturepedic. However, for 1985 Zweig's recommendations are likely to be extraordinarily good, as they were in '81 and '82; or else not so good, as they were in '83; or else kind of rotten, as they were on rare occasion way back when. Who knows? *The Option Advisor,* reports Hulbert in his digest, was up a spectacular 97.9 percent in the first quarter of 1984 ($225 a year, Box 46709, Cincinnati, Ohio 45246). On the other hand, it was down 93.4 percent in 1983. So, if you'd invested $10,000 according to its recommendations in 1983, you'd have been down to about $660 by the start of 1984, and then that $660 would have doubled.

And how can we forget Joe ("I can never be wrong again") Granville, whose market-shaking predictions you could have received for $250 a year, or, when he was really hot, by watching the nightly news? Granville was great for a while, except that those who stuck with his advice would ultimately have been taken to the cleaners. ("My name's Granville, not God," he eventually shrugged.)

Howard Ruff has a newsletter. Subscribe and you get a free LP, on which Howard sings "If I Were a Rich Man," "Hymn to America," "I Walked Today Where Jesus Walked," "My Way," "Climb Every Mountain" and "The Impossible Dream" . . . and/or copies of all Howard's outdated hardcover books. The newsletter is largely occupied with introducing additions to the Ruff family (he has 30 or 40 kids), spurring readers to political action (he has his own lobbying organ), and promoting new or affiliated newsletters. He has great skills as a communicator and marketer, substantial skill as a singer and financial analyst.

He will start one newsletter with an anonymous, and possibly fabricated, letter so he can defend free enterprise and the profit motive ("Dear Howard: Why are you always trying to sell us other newsletters, coins, books and cruises? All you care about is getting rich. You're greedy"). He starts another by chewing out impatient subscribers who wonder why gold and silver *still* haven't gone up. The mystery of it is that he actually has more than 150,000 fans paying $89 a year (and more) to cheer him on.

He's the misunderstood multimillionaire underdog, fighting valiantly against the big bad Government, and the fact that his investment advice is sometimes good, sometimes not so good, is almost beside the point. It's you and him against the establishment, you and him against the Russians, you and him against the welfare cheats, you and him against Congress (well, he's got a point there), you and him against promiscuity, you and him against impatient, ungrateful subscribers.

You and he on exotic, arguably tax-deductible investment seminar tours. You and he assuring his next book, *Making Money,* climbs to #1 on the best-seller list, thereby confirming his popularity and expertise. ("Buy the book sometime in the two weeks beginning May 14," he offered 175,000 subscribers, and your newsletter subscription will be extended at no charge.)

The investment letters I do like don't attempt to predict world events, the price of gold or even the course of the stock market, but provide the kind of fundamental analysis on overlooked or undervalued situations I don't have time to do. And even then I don't have a great deal of confidence in them, because picking undervalued stocks is a tough, tough game. Most people will be better off picking a seasoned mutual fund that picks undervalued stocks, like Mutual Shares Corporation (26 Broadway, New York, NY 10004).

For those who'd rather do it themselves, the *Value Line Investment Survey* (711 Third Avenue, New York, NY 10017) may be worth a trial subscription. Two upstart newsletters for the small investor to which you might write requesting sample copies are *BI Research* (Box 301, South Salem, NY 10590) and *FXC Investors* (62-19 Cooper Avenue, Glendale, NY 11385). More widely known are Charles Allmon's *Growth Stock Outlook* (Box 15381, Chevy Chase, MD 20815) and *Market Logic* (3471 North Federal Highway, Ft. Lauderdale, FL 33306). Just keep in mind that this is a tough, tough game to win.

Generally, when asked where to look for sound investment ideas, I suggest a subscription to *Forbes*. But that's no good because no one expects to get rich fast reading *Forbes*. We *want* to believe there's a simple, worry-free way to make 1,555 percent on our money. And I don't blame us.

14

IS THE STOCK MARKET FOR YOU?
Getting Rich Maybe

The best performing stock groups in 1949 were the leathers, the utilities, the papers and the soaps. The Dow Jones Industrial Average hovered above 160. Inflation was running at 2.7 percent—"intolerable," Thomas Dewey called it—and 40 percent of Americans believed a new depression was in the making. Of 375 middle-class Los Angeles families polled, only seven could name a single brokerage house.

And out of all this was born the grandest, most munificent, sweeping, soaring, rip-snorting bull market the country has ever known.

The Last Bull Market, by Robert Sobel (the ambiguity in the title was deliberate), published in 1980, can't qualify as one of the greatest money books ever published (chapter 10), but it does provide readers new to Wall Street and the economy with twenty-odd years of you-were-there background. For those who *were* there, it offers nostalgia, amusement and perspective.

There's no getting around it: hindsight is fun. (One analyst in 1957 described Polaroid as "an interesting toy company, but no more than that."

Sobel takes us through the Eisenhower years, during which Walter Winchell was reduced to touting stocks to boost his ratings. "After each broadcast some of his listeners would act on his advice, and the prices of these stocks would rise. He would take note of this the following week and make new recommendations. . . . Perhaps without meaning to do so, he served as a pied-piper luring small-time speculators to the Street."

And in they came, rising from fewer than 5 million shareholders to 30 million as the economy boomed through the fifties and sixties and the market boomed with it. Mutual fund sales burgeoned; "institutions" began trading so heavily in their quest for "performance" that they came to dominate the market (rising from 22 percent of New York Stock Exchange volume in 1961 to 60 percent eight years later). Money managers were "gunslingers"; conglomerateurs were kings. There were the fall-out shelters, the Berlin Wall, the Bay of Pigs, Kennedy vs. Big Steel, "peace scares" (if you owned General Dynamics, peace was scary), stocks of absurd little companies that doubled in their first day of trading, the chicken franchisers (Hungarian Fried Chicken was to be the Gabor sisters' chain), and people saying the most outlandish things. (" 'We aim at a 30 percent growth rate for our clients' assets,' said one money manager in 1965, adding quickly, 'Of course we expect to do better than that overall, but 30 percent is the rock bottom.' ")

Johnson came to view the Dow as a measure of his popularity, even as he was digging away the foundations of the bull market with his policies. Writes Sobel: "Sometime in the summer of 1966, the champagne went flat on Wall Street. The joy and verve, the spirit of innovation and risk—and even the reckless daring . . . faded or changed into little more than a jaded opportunism." "Inflation was in the air" that year (it had risen past 3 percent). To deal with it, the Fed was putting on the screws. On March 10, 1966, Morgan Guaranty raised its prime lending rate to an astonishing 5½ percent, "a level that had not been seen since the bleakest days of the Hoover years." Other banks followed. Stocks plummeted.

In those days, however, declines were shortlived, rallies powerful. Not until the last month of 1968 would this great twenty-year bull market—well, simply peter out. There was no dramatic sell-off, and it was certainly not apparent at the time; but at the end of 1968, with the Dow just shy of 1,000, it was over. Fourteen years later—the summer of 1982—adjusted for inflation, the Dow was in the high 200s.

The next several years could be great ones to own common stocks. Even so, the stock market may not be for you.

Until you've paid off your high-interest loans, purchased the insurance protection you need (if any), and stashed $5,000 or $10,000 someplace safe, like a bank, it's crazy even to *think* about the stock market. Immediately this is depressing.

Yet if you don't meet these criteria, be consoled. First, you'll save time and emotional energy. Investing—especially sensible investing—is not without its demands. Second, you won't lose money. The chances are all too good, especially if you're a little leaguer (and for all I know, you're Babe Ruth), that's just what would have happened to you.

You would have bought 100 shares of Pan Am at 9, as a major brokerage firm recommended at the end of 1983, because for a mere $935 (with the commission) you could buy a full 100 shares. A certain satisfaction comes with owning shares in the nation's flagship airline, with its dynamic new chief executive, as recommended by one of the nation's most highly regarded brokerage firms. (I'd rather not tell you which one it is, but when this outfit talks, people listen.) Eight months later, with Pan Am at 4¼, you would have tired of waiting for your money to multiply and sold out your position ($390 after the commission) to buy a TV.

Or if it wasn't Pan Am, it would have been options. As you know, there's a booming business in stock options. You buy a "call" option on GM if you expect GM stock to rise sharply over the next several weeks; a "put" if you expect a sharp decline. The great thing about options is that they don't cost much.

A gentleman I know recently turned $400 into $18,000 in four months trading options. Turning $400 into $18,000 is something many of us would like to do. (And if $400 can become $18,000, cannot $4,000 just as easily become $180,000?) But I'm not going to tell you how he did it (he had a simple system) because, first, you might not be able to execute the system with the same skill he did—this man graduated from college with high honors and spends his *life* in the financial markets—and, second, in the fifth and sixth months, with the same system, he lost the full $18,000 and then some.

Unless you are a professional trader with a mainframe computer and no brokerage commissions to pay, playing the stock option game is gambling pure and simple. It has nothing to do with investing. Rather, it's a zero-sum game, meaning that for each dollar won a dollar is lost. Only, because of brokerage commissions and taxes, it's really a *sub*-zero sum game. For each $1 won, *$1.10* is lost. Play long enough and you will lose. It's that simple. (For bigger players, options can serve a risk-limiting function, but that's another story.)

Playing the stock market is somewhat less risky than playing with options, but involves much the same thing: lots of trades and brokerage commissions; heavy taxes if you get lucky and win.

Investing in the stock market—seeking exceptional values when the market is depressed and holding them for years—can be different. Few commissions; lots of dividends; light taxes on long-term capital gains. Investing need not be a zero-sum game, because over time the entire economy can prosper, and its owners with it.

But prudence is boring; financial ferreting takes effort and at least a little expertise. It's a lot more fun to hear a hot story in the locker room and take a flier.

So one fundamental question to answer is whether you want to have a little fun playing the market and likely lose money; or go the boring, effortful way and maybe make a little. When the question is posed this way, almost everyone chooses the second answer. When it is posed by real life, we often choose the first.

And there are other questions. Let's assume you can afford the risks of the stock market. Do you have the temperament for it?

Think about it: Would you be comfortable buying stocks when things are awful and most people are convinced they'll get worse? Would you have the discipline to sell your winners when everything's going great? It's not easy!

And would you perhaps feel a little "guilty" if you did win big? If you actually turned $7,500 into $13,000 in a month with no tangible effort on your part? You'd be thrilled—but would you feel a tinge of guilt? If so, your subconscious may work against you. There's an element of self-destructiveness in us all. The bigger yours is, the further from the stock market you should steer.

If you can afford to invest in the stock market, and if you do have the time and temperament, there's a final question:

Can you beat it? Can you do any better than average? For if you can't, why bother to do it yourself? Why not invest through one or a couple of professionally managed mutual funds?

A lot of study has shown that *very* few individual investors or brokers (or professionally managed mutual funds) can do consistently better than average, any more than they could predict the flip of a coin with better than 50 percent accuracy. Success in the market isn't completely random; but to do even 3 or 4 percent a year better than average—up 13 percent when the market as a whole is up 10 percent, down 7 percent when the market's down 10 percent—is extraordinarily tough. Especially after you take brokerage commissions into account. Sure, you might beat the pants off the market one year. But that hardly helps if you get creamed the next.

There are two basic possibilities (with the truth, as usual, lying someplace in between). Interestingly, both possibilities point to more or less the same conclusion:

• If hard work, high intelligence and years of experience *do* help to do well in the stock market, then you're up against some extraordinary competition. Why fight it, when for a very modest fee you can avail yourself of professional management by investing through a mutual fund? It's true that as a little guy you may be able to find crevices of nimble opportunity the big mutual funds can't fit into; but it's also true that it's easier to be patient, and to diversify, when you're sitting on $100 million than when you're sitting on $5,237.93.

• If hard work, high intelligence and years of experience *don't* help to do well in the market—if, that is, the proverbial dart-flinging monkey* can do just as well as most pros, as more than a little evidence suggests he can—then how you do in the market is largely a matter of how well the market itself does. When it rises, you'll rise; when it falls, you'll fall. If trying doesn't help, why try? Again: invest through mutual funds. (And if you really think you can predict the course of the market, switch into aggressive funds when it's poised to rise; into money market funds when it's poised to fall. Two newsletters that attempt to guide you in this manner are the *Telephone Switch Newsletter,* in Huntington Beach, California, and the *Switch Fund Advisory,* in Gaithersburg, Maryland.)

Over time, investments in the stock market are well re-

---

* I say proverbial because I've spent several hours trying to get a chimpanzee to throw darts, which the chimp, even for $750 and with the help of two trainers banging him on the head, proved unable to do. He was much better in the role of psychiatrist, sitting behind me and taking notes on a yellow legal pad.

warded. The average return from stocks has historically been higher than the return from safer investments—and, speaking very broadly, this is likely to be the case in the future—because over the long term the market rewards risk.

All I ask is that you take a look to see whether you're in the market in a casual way to have a little fun, and maybe get lucky —which is fine, if that's what you want to do—or whether you're in it in a serious way to provide for your future security. If it's the latter, ask yourself whether your interests wouldn't be better served by a long-term program of regular monthly investments in one or more broad-based, sensibly managed no-load mutual funds.

An excellent source of information on the ins and outs of selecting mutual funds is *The 1984 Handbook for No-Load Fund Investors* (Box 283 Hastings-on-Hudson, New York 10706—$29). Be sure to choose funds that have done well in both up and down cycles of the market. A fund that's done great over the last couple of years is often exactly the one about to do poorly over the next couple, as the cycle shifts.

To understand cycles, and the big picture, I once had an opportunity to spend a couple of hours at the feet of the second most powerful man in the country. Although the audience was granted in 1982, the things I learned seem no less apt—and encouraging—today.

15

MR. MONEY EXPLAINS IT ALL
A Conversation with the Chairman of the Board

There would seem to be little doubt that the second most powerful man in the country since 1979 has been Paul Volcker, chairman of the Board of Governors of the Federal Reserve System. In June 1982, when he sat for his first extended interview since becoming chairman of the Fed three years earlier, the U.S. was in the midst of a truly grave economic mess. Yet even then, with the stock market dismally low and headed lower, with unemployment high and headed higher, with interest rates stuck in what some considered an impossible gridlock —even then, Volcker made a strong case that much of the worst was behind us. That this decade, if we keep our wits about us, could become the mirror image of the last one: a decade of *falling* inflation, *falling* interest rates, *rising* productivity, *rising* real wages, *falling* unemployment.

Given today's improved but still precarious environment, it sounds almost too good to be true. Is it possible things could actually go right for a change?

"This is not an impossible vision," Volcker has said. "Much of the groundwork has been laid."

There has been the Fed's own restrictive monetary policy—a steady "leaning against the wind" of inflation—which Volcker has consistently vowed to continue. There have been, too, moves toward deregulation, a moderating in the demands of labor, and changes in the tax code to encourage investment (two important results: a boom in venture capital and some 20 million individual retirement accounts set up since 1981).

"Today," Volcker said in June 1982, "we are acutely aware of disturbed capital markets, high interest rates, economic slack, and poor productivity. But when the economy begins to expand, productivity should rise. That, in turn, will permit prices to rise more slowly than wages, encouraging further moderation in wage demands." And further disinflation. "As confidence returns to securities markets, prices of bonds and stocks should rise. Lower interest rates will, in turn, support the continuing growth in investment and productivity." Things could gradually get better and better. "With appropriate budgetary and monetary discipline, the process could be sustained for years."

"What we're aiming for," said Volcker, "is a situation in which people can proceed about their business without worrying about what prices are going to do over the next year, two years, three years, ten years, and can take it for granted that they're going to be more or less stable—where it's not a factor that they should spend a lot of time worrying about in their investment decisions or consumption decisions. And in that kind of environment you ought to have the kind of interest rates we had in the mid '60s, anyway."

The prime rate, in 1965 averaged 4½ percent. Municipal bonds yielded 3¼ percent. Home mortgages were still under 6 percent, as they had been, with only minor exceptions, for more than a century.

WHAT THE FED DOES

In the broadest sense, the principal responsibility of the nation's central bank is to see to the health of the national currency: the dollar. Inflation wrecks a nation's currency, and the inflation Mr. Volcker inherited on August 6, 1979, was of a type so prolonged and virulent that many young Americans—as he frequently points out—have never *not* known it.

Ordinarily, faced with economic and social chaos—for this is what prolonged, accelerating inflation inevitably brings—both the monetary and fiscal instruments of economic policy would be brought sharply to bear: the Fed would get tough, which it has; and so would the administration and the Congress, which have, instead, given us $200 billion deficits. In a recession, such deficits, given the size of our economy, should be tolerable. (Like a family that spends more than it earns for a while after one spouse has been laid off.) But it was projected that the deficit would expand even *with* an economic recovery. (Like a family that spends a lot more than it earns *all* the time.)

One best-selling doomsayer thus described the Fed's efforts, which he lauded, as "one hand clapping." Buy gold, he advised in the spring of 1982, the next round of inflation will be much worse. ("Is he *still* saying that?" Volcker asked me.)

Perhaps by the time you read this that next round of inflation will be well underway. If not—if the cycle of ever worsening inflation followed by ever more desperate recession has been broken—it will largely be attributable to the efforts of the Fed.

THE FED'S PROBLEM

There are lots of complicated technical things the Fed can do to "administer monetary policy," but really they boil down to two: the Fed can ease up, by expanding the money supply; or tighten up, by restricting it.

Here's the way it's supposed to work: if the Fed pumps money into the system, interest rates—the price of money—fall. (Money is like anything else. When you increase its supply, its price falls.) Lower interest rates allow more people to buy cars and houses; business booms; unemployment falls; tax receipts rise; everything is wonderful.

Except that if you pump money into the economy faster than is needed to keep up with real growth, you fuel inflation. Pumping new dollars into the system cheapens those already in existence.

So what had begun to happen by the summer of 1982 was that when the financial markets (which include anyone with a few dollars to invest) perceived an easing in money, they feared a new round of inflation—and interest rates rose.

Great! Tighten up on money and interest rates rise; ease up —and they rise, too! This leaves not a lot of room for maneuver.

The trick is for the Fed to be able to ease up a bit, occasionally, as conditions warrant, while persuading the financial markets that the fundamental anti-inflationary policy has not been abandoned.

It's not enough simply to say the policy has not been abandoned. We've been through too much to believe all the pronouncements of our elected and appointed officials. That only worked in a simpler, more innocent time. Anyone who bought 8½ percent thirty-year bonds in 1976, when inflation had been damped down from double digits to a mere 5 percent, trusting promises of a sound dollar ever after, carries a deep scar. Volcker appreciates the problem. Credibility must be *earned,* he constantly reasserts, by persistence and performance.

"The only way that confidence and, therefore, moderate and stable interest rates can be restored," Ashby Bladen, author of *How to cope with the Developing Financial Crisis,* has written, "is through a long period of responsible and noninflationary policies."

You've seen the "Peanuts" classic. Lucy's index finger is on a football awaiting Charlie Brown's big toe. "Come on, Charlie Brown—kick it!" she says. Charlie Brown says no. "Come on, Charlie Brown," she says—"*kick* it!" Every year Lucy plays this dumb trick on him. Just as he runs to the ball and begins to kick she whisks the ball away and he falls *boink!* on his head. This year, he tells her, he's not going to fall for it. Lucy swears up and down that this year she'll really hold the ball—ascribes past behavior to immaturity, since outgrown—but Charlie Brown shakes his head. "I *swear* I won't pull the ball away," she says. "I *swear!*" This year, she means it. She really, really means it. So, trusting soul, Charlie Brown runs up to the ball, kicks his little heart out—and lands on his head. Lucy laughs hysterically.

"Is it fair to say," Volcker is asked, "that this is the nub of the whole thing? That your very biggest problem, in a way, is somehow convincing the financial markets that you really, really mean it?"

"Yes. Without killing the economy in the process."

This is the Fed's biggest problem. It has others.

WHAT'S MONEY?

The Fed is charged with managing the money supply. Okay —what's money? Cash, of course, and checking account balances. But do you include money market funds? Savings accounts? Savings certificates? Savings bonds? (Corporate bonds? Stocks? Options? Diamonds? Stamps? Baseball cards?) How about borrowing power?

It used to be that the only way to buy something was to have coins in your pocket. Someone with no coins had no money. Today, someone with no coins but $2,000 of unused credit on his MasterCard can buy $2,000 worth of goods. Is that credit line "money"?

Ultimately, technically, says Volcker, you could get to the point where nobody keeps any cash or checking-account balance at all. Everybody runs an overdraft all the time. "Then what do you call the money supply? The total of their overdraft limits?"

"Basically, we've got a problem interpreting what's going on ourselves," Fed governor Nancy Hays Teeters told the *New York Times* at the time of my interview with Volcker. Echoed Federal Reserve Bank of Boston President Frank E. Morris: "I have . . . concluded, most reluctantly, that we can no longer measure the money supply with any kind of precision . . ."

If you can't define it or measure it, how do you control it? Said Morris: "We are in a Catch-22 situation in that the one thing we are well positioned to control"—cash and bank reserves—"is no longer a meaningful target for monetary policy."

And yet for all the difficulty in defining, measuring and controlling the money supply (thereby to maintain stable prices, a stable currency, and the American Way of Life), Volcker believes it can still be done. "Obviously," he says, "our presumption is you can do it within a narrow enough band—which is not as narrow as some people think it is—in a way that's meaningful in today's conditions. But I don't think you can just write a rule that's supposed to last for ten years or something." Particularly when times are tough and the Fed has the squeeze on, everybody has a rule he'd like to write into law that would work for ten years.

What many fail to grasp is that economics works less neatly in the real world than in textbooks. It's one thing to get a couple of chemicals to react the way you want them to. People are less predictable. You can regulate taxes and government spending and the number of dollar bills in circulation, for example—all important influences on economic activity—but how do you regulate confidence?

Consider: if the projected budget deficits were smaller, interest rates would be lower (because Treasury borrowing and inflationary expectations would ease). Yet if only interest rates were lower, the budget deficit *would* be smaller (because tax receipts would be higher; expenditures lower)!

It is one of those circular problems very much on the order of, "All we have to fear is fear itself." The 1982 version (which, in lesser degree, still applied in 1984): "If we had confidence inflation were over (and consequently moderated our wage demands, committed our money to productive long-term investments, and so forth), inflation *would* end."

And yet, one Fed governor acknowledged, ". . . you can push the economy so hard to kill inflation that you discourage the investment that killing inflation was meant to stimulate."

So the Fed in June 1982 was in an impossible box: push too hard and a flood of massive bankruptcies could deepen the recession, lead to even more horrendous deficits and perhaps even higher interest rates. Or, if the Fed stepped in to avert massive bankruptcies, pumping vast billions into the system, that, too, could send inflation and interest rates through the roof.

As the economists at Aetna Life & Casualty put it that summer: "Our central bankers have so far engineered the economy along the razor's edge between reinflation and financial chaos. The more doctrinaire monetarists may call this irresponsible. We prefer to call it the application of reasoned human judgment."

CIGARS, CIGARETTES, TIPARILLOS?

Given the extraordinary difficulties Volcker has faced, and still faces, as chairman of the Fed, it is hard not to wonder whether he actually likes his job. "Do you *like* this job?" I ask him as he settles his six feet seven inches onto the couch under one of two large paintings in his office (a farmhouse, by the wife of the staff director for monetary and financial policy). He is wearing a banker's pin-striped suit, white shirt, laced black shoes, and has a sharp pencil sticking out of the pocket a dandier soul might use to display a handkerchief.

The question makes him laugh. The second most powerful man in America has a voice like the largest drum in the band, tapped gently, for the most part; and an almost Santalike laugh. He is entirely forthcoming.

"I don't think of it in those terms," he says, "I really don't. I know some people say, 'Gee is it exciting?' or 'Are you having fun?'—that's a favorite remark—and I suppose in some deeper sense you are, but" (his voice rises to a low boom as he laughs) "I don't think of it as fun on a day-to-day BA-A-sis! There's a satisfaction, I guess, but it seems to me you do it because it's here, and you got picked."

Mr. Volcker was picked by Jimmy Carter to succeed the undistinguished chairmanship of G. William Miller (1978–79), who had succeeded Arthur Burns (1970–78), who had succeeded William McChesney Martin, Jr. (1951–70). There were Fed chairmen before Bill Martin—Charles Hamlin, in 1914, was the first—but that's not important. Not important, either, but the principal way the public has perceived these men: Burns smoked a pipe, Miller smoked nothing and posted a sign requesting the same of his colleagues (to mixed reviews), and Volcker smokes Antony & Cleopatra Grenadiers, $1.45 the half dozen.

Periodically as he speaks, legs outstretched on the sofa, he will absentmindedly wave a match in the air to extinguish it, then toss it into a large pewter ashtray. (Around its rim: "When You Leave New York, You Ain't Going Nowhere.") Still smoldering, the match bounces out onto the hardwood coffee table. Again and again, his interviewer reaches over to make the save. Volcker played basketball for Princeton, but only second string. Now his sport is fishing. This *is* important, as it reflects one of his principal attributes: patience. Two others: consistency and, as one senator put it near the end of a 190-minute subcommittee grilling, "coolness under fire."

THE MESS IN 1979

Volcker did not arrive in Washington thinking he had all the answers. "In a very general way, I thought I had some sense of what the problems were," he says; "it's a field I've been in virtually all my life. But I did not have the sense that this was an ideal time to become chairman of the board from the standpoint of an easy time! And," he smiles, "it's fully lived up to that!"

Prior to assuming the chairmanship, he had presided over the Federal Reserve Bank of New York. There he earned $116,000. As chairman of the entire twelve-bank system, he earns $72,200, up from $60,600 in 1982. For this princely stipend, some would say, he bears the weight of the Western World on his shoulders (the Europeans are often mad at him, too). But Paul Volcker, fifty-seven, does not appear to be a man raw from criticism or awesomely burdened. He has no great difficulty sleeping. "I see myself to a considerable extent as part of an institution," he says. "And not just the institution of the Federal Reserve, but in a broader sense you're part of a bigger governmental apparatus. I don't personalize it as much as people outside do." Like the 2,000 construction industry executives, four or five years ago, who slapped $1.81 in postage on blocks of two-by-four, addressed them to Paul A. Volcker, ink on wood, and dropped them in the mail. "I've become the symbol for monetary policy. Maybe I don't feel quite as burdened as I might if I really had all the power people think I have."

Born in Cape May, New Jersey, Volcker went to Princeton, to Harvard and to the London School of Economics. From there he went to work for the Fed, for Chase Manhattan, for the Treasury, for Chase Manhattan again, for the Treasury again (as under secretary for Monetary Affairs) and then spent a year at Princeton's Woodrow Wilson School. In August 1975 he was tapped to run the Federal Reserve Bank of New York. Four years later he became chairman of the Fed.

The situation he inherited was alarming. We all lived through this period from the outside; take a few minutes to relive it, or at least its highlights, from the inside, from the perspective of the chairman of the Fed. "You had a sense in the summer of '79," he says, "that psychologically and otherwise inflation was getting ahead of us. I suppose we're interested in inflation in the end because the economy over a long period of time can't operate very well without a stable currency.

"So more forceful action probably had to be taken, and it was only a couple of months after I was here that we adopted this new operating technique—I'm not sure we understood all the implications, you never do, but we understood some of them, certainly."

The new technique was a major refocusing. Rather than influence the money supply, and hence the economy, by managing the level of interest rates, as it had done in the past, the Fed announced in October 1979 it would henceforth concentrate on controlling the money supply directly, letting interest rates fall —or rise—where they may.

"What we did was not basically a new idea. It had been kicking around. I'd thought about it some, but I can't say I'd been an advocate of it. I thought it had some problems. What persuaded me personally was the need to somehow get a grip on the situation, and on psychology, and this seemed to me a way to do it.

"We had taken some tightening moves in August/September that didn't seem to make much of an impact. So I thought, you know, how can we change the approach a little bit here to get people's a-TE-EN-tion!" Mr. Volcker's laughter erupts through his words in capital letters.

"One of the things we did anticipate—that it would inject more instability into the market in the short run—was not considered altogether undesirable at that point. A little more uncertainty, we thought, might have favorable effects on psychology and behavior, speculative behavior in particular."

Gold had nearly doubled in the previous year and its rise was accelerating. In California, people were buying extra houses to capitalize on inflation. From going largely unnoticed a decade earlier, inflation had become so entrenched that middle America was devising schemes to profit from it.

The Fed's refocusing was initially well received. "It was highly successful in the sense of conveying to the public the idea of what we wanted to do and getting some understanding, as much as any of these things can," says Volcker. The dollar stabilized. But interest rates proved even more volatile than the Fed had anticipated—and rose higher.

CREDIT CONTROLS IN 1980

The Fed's second big move came in March 1980: the imposition of controls on consumer credit. In hindsight, not such a great idea.

"I think cer-ERtainly, with the benefit of hindsight, we would have done a few things differently during this period!" booms Volcker. At the time, though, *something* had to be done. Inflation was raging at an 18 percent annual rate. "Despite what we had done up to that point, people had gotten more scared than they were before, I think.

"And you kept getting reports from the market that interest rates may be high, but everybody wants to lend like crazy, nobody wants to restrain anything, they're all looking to more inflation. So the general idea of maybe having to do something more forceful was not foreign to me.

"The President wanted to put together a big program, which I was encouraging him to do."

But what Carter came up with was a plan to limit the growth in consumer credit. Volcker didn't like the idea.

"I did not want to invoke the Credit Control Act. I thought it was very much a two-edged sword. You never know what the results of these sorts of things are going to be, and it raises the question—well, they're talking about some narrow sector of consumer credit, but what specter is that going to raise in everybody's mind?" Federally mandated credit allocation? Interest rate controls? "But we finally went along with it. The President wanted to invoke the Act and we would have had a confrontation if we refused to administer it. So we agreed to do something in the consumer credit area and we found out that it had a lot bigger psychological repercussion than we or the administration had assumed."

The Fed took the mildest action it could think of. Banks, department stores and credit card companies were told that to the extent they allowed consumer loans to increase, they would have to pay a small penalty, which they could pass on to their customers or not as they saw fit. (Most saw fit.) Secured loans, for things like cars and houses, were not included.

"In economic terms it was a small action," Volker says, "but when the President of the United States announces we don't want people using their credit cards, and that measures would be taken, the sheer confusion and message that came through was: 'Don't use consumer credit!' Including automobile credit and that kind of stuff, which we'd exempted. And you got a very sharp reaction in the economy."

It plunged.

"It looked like a recession, and it went down in the history books as a recession, but I guess in retrospect it was an odd kind of contrived affair. We lifted those controls as soon as it looked reasonable to do so, because we didn't want them on any longer than we had to. It was always in my mind they'd be temporary.''

Imposed March 14, 1980, the controls were partially dismantled ten weeks later and gone entirely by July 4. But if Volcker and his six fellow Fed governors knew the controls would be fleeting, the public was less sure.

"The people who were really worried were the retailers—and it became quite clear why. They were worried about the Christmas season, when you get a big seasonal increase in consumer credit.

"Well, I must confess it was a problem we had not thought about, because I know in all my thinking I did not imagine the controls would still be in place nine months later during the CHRI-Istmas season! I always saw them as very temporary—I hadn't given a bit of thought to the Christmas season. But from their standpoint, they had to begin planning, and it was a perfectly natural concern.

"But anyhow, the economy had this abrupt fall, and the money supply fell very rapidly with it. It was an artificial reaction precisely to the consumer credit controls. Consumers suddenly thought they'd better not use consumer credit, so they drew down their cash balances. So you had this wild decline for six weeks or so in the money supply. Interest rates fell like a stone, too.''

And why not? The demand for credit had been suddenly stifled—and when the demand for something falls, so does its price. But the action backfired.

"In a sense you had the psychological result that everybody says—'The problem's over with.' The basic problem of inflation was *not* over with,'' but once the credit restrictions were lifted it seemed as if "restrictive policies were no longer in fashion, everything was easy again—business as usual,'' says Volcker. "We lost some psychological ground.''

The money supply began rising again. "It began bouncing back, which we didn't mind for a month or two because it was just offsetting the decline. What we did not judge, we nor any-body else, was that the economic decline itself was going to be so short-lived. It was not a popularly held forecast.''

The Fed kept expecting growth in the money supply to slow down—but it didn't.

''And part of the reason it didn't,'' says Volcker, ''was that the economy was picking up much faster than people were assuming. The thing got a degree of momentum over the next six months that in hindsight was psychologically damaging. If it hadn't been the focus of so much attention, I don't think it would have made much difference, but everybody had come to look at the money supply figures as the symbol of policy. And we were in the midst of an election campaign, so everybody could attribute political interpretations to everything that hap-pened. That didn't help any.''

Down from near 20 percent in April 1980 to 11 percent by August, the prime was back to 20 percent by December.

''The net of that long story is that I think the kind of discon-tinuity introduced by the credit controls was harmful rather than helpful.''

PSYCHOLOGY

The net of that long story may also be that chairing the Fed and charting appropriate monetary policy have as much to do with psychology as with finance.

''You do get caught in that dilemma,'' Volcker acknowl-edges. ''Sometimes the technical analysis runs in the same di-rection as what the psychology seems to be telling you''—so making policy is easy—''but sometimes they run in opposite directions. Then they do create a dilemma. And the psychology often runs to extremes. You go back to early '80—I mean, people were really scared! 'The Federal Reserve isn't restric-tive at all, this thing is never gonna stop, credit expansion is gonna go on forever'—and of course within three weeks the view was all changed, but that was the psychology that existed. And you're tempted, sometimes rightly, sometimes maybe wrongly, to respond to the psychology. Sometimes I think you have to. But on purely technical grounds it can be a mistake to do it—and that creates a great dilemma.

"Sometimes it means there is no right policy, I think. You know, what seems technically right *isn't* right if the psychology is running in the other direction and it makes no impact. It can be very hard to deal with in the short run."

You can do all the sensible technical things, but if you can't persuade the marketplace of your long-term intentions and resolve, you've failed. But how do you persuade the marketplace "without killing the economy in the process?"

"That's the basic dilemma. You've got so much underlying inflationary momentum, exaggerated at times, but it's clearly there—reality I'm talking about now . . ." Wages really *had* been rocketing. Productivity really *had* stagnated. We really *had* suffered from a degree of managerial complacency born of decades of world economic superiority. People really *had* bet on continued inflation. "All this comes along and collides with a restrictive monetary posture, sooner or later, and there is a kind of real collision if there isn't enough money to permit this momentum to continue. There's a kind of psychological collision, too, because behavior doesn't change very readily. And if people don't believe that you're going to carry thrOU-U-gh, it'll change all the more slowly!

"But if it changes *too* slowly," Volcker says quietly, "then you got an impossible problem." Long pause.

BACK TO A GOLD STANDARD?

As it turned out, we squeaked by. What could have turned into an economic cataclysm in 1982 turned, instead, into a couple of very favorable years. But it's far from clear that inflation is a thing of the past—and was even further from clear in the summer of 1982. Back then it was not even clear whether Volcker would be reappointed chairman when his term expired in August 1983. (Fed governors serve twelve-year terms. The chairman's job runs for four. Had Volcker not been reappointed chairman, he could have continued to serve as a governor, but it was assumed he'd move on.)

To get people to believe the Fed would really carry through —that it really, really meant it—what would Paul Volcker think, I wondered, of Reagan's announcing a year in advance that he'd be reappointed? The chairman snorted in amusement and relit his cigar, bouncing a smoldering match out of the ashtray onto the table for his interviewer to rescue.

"People reach out and try to think of something that's gonna symbolize what you're after," he says. "I think that's the root of the interest in the gold standard. You're saying, in effect, how about 'a Volcker standard.' Or other people would say, write in a monetary rule." (By which Congress would set by law, today, the rate at which the money supply would be allowed to grow in the future.)

"I *wish* it were that SI-IMple," he laughs, "but I don't think we're gonna win it just by hanging out some dramatic symbolic action, whatever that action is. That's the basic trouble with the gold standard thing—there are lots of technical troubles, but the trouble with that argument is: great, we're going on the gold standard, therefore thirty-year bond rates are going to go down to 5 percent because they know we're on the gold standard. But they know much more than that! We went *off* the gold standard ten years ago, and there's nothing to prevent . . . You know, once you've bit the apple, you can't say you haven't left the Garden of Eden.

"I'm not a disbeliever in all symbolism; in fact, to an extent I believe in symbolism. The older I get, the more importance I think there is in just conveying a message to the public. You've got to keep things simple. Half of this dilemma is trying to keep things simple enough to be understood, so it will affect people's behavior, without getting caught by the simplicity of what you're SAY-AYing, and having the real world jump up and bite you."

You've also got to take account of political realities.

"I think these criticisms that the Federal Reserve was a great engine of inflation are really unfair," Volcker says. "An institution does what it can within the framework of a big environment."

The Fed is independent by law, but laws can be changed.

"Well, I suppose it's that concern put in its crudest form," Volker says, "but you don't even have to put it that way. It's not that Congress goes and legislates a different policy, which is the ultimate possibility. Your policy itself is not going to be successful if you haven't got a reasonable degree of understanding around the country of what you're trying to do, and a kind of willingness to support it. I'm not saying you have to have a majority vote. You can have a lot of opposition. But I don't think you can sustain a policy whose purpose no one understands. So you've got to operate under that general constraint, if for no other reason than if they don't understand it, they don't think it's going to last. Which is where you come back to your psychological point—getting people to believe."

THE VELOCITY OF MONEY

With everyone in the "big environment" screaming about interest rates, the task in the gridlocked summer of '82 was to ease up, insofar as might be justified, without reigniting inflation. It was a two-part effort. First you had to figure out how much easing was justified; then you had to get the financial markets to "agree."

One might imagine, for example, that when the stock market

takes a frightening plunge, the money supply has in a sense plunged, too. Stockholders feel poorer, have less to borrow against, and so spend less freely.

"I wouldn't call it the money supply or even the credit supply, but I agree that it's a factor," says Volcker. "The big engine for this kind of stuff has not been stocks recently, but houses—where everybody began taking out their equity with second mortgages, convinced that that equity was going to increase forever and ever."

So hadn't the drop in real estate values given the Fed a legitimate rationale to pump up the money supply, just by way of compensation?

"Yeah, if we just looked at that I think it is accurate. But here's precisely where we get into the problem. Suppose your analysis is exactly right—there's something to it, anyway. So we could say, 'Look, people are going to spend less money and they're going to want higher cash balances because the value of their houses has gone down, so we think precisely the right thing to do is—where we said we were going to increase the money supply by 5 percent, we've now recalibrated that at 7½ percent.' *How do you explain that?*

"Hey, we've got that problem right now! It's a more general phenomenon, but it's not unrelated to yours: people want to be more liquid. And part of being more liquid is holding more money in the bank. It's very easy to relate it to fear about the recession, fear about the financial system—people want to hold more money.

"Now, if that phenomenon is going on, and there's no doubt in my mind that it is, then I think it's true to say you would not want the money supply to be as low as it otherwise would have been, because in economic terms you're being tighter than you intended. But try to quantify that and try to explain it!"

(The more work any given dollar bill can do in a year—the more hands it can pass through—the greater its "velocity." And the more work dollars do, the fewer of them the economy needs. So when velocity increases, the money supply in a sense increases, too, even though the actual number of dollars in circulation may have remained constant. By moving around faster, they can handle an expanded level of transactions. To conduct monetary policy, therefore, you must not only "count" the number of dollars in the money supply—you've got to figure out how fast they're moving.)

It is doubtless a sound economic notion: that dollars frozen in the checking accounts of people too scared to spend or invest them pass through fewer hands, support less economic activity, than dollars that move around faster. But can the Fed announce an easing in monetary policy based on such a thing?

Every Thursday just past four, East Coast time, men and women throughout the nation and much of the world stop what they're doing to await the weekly money supply figures (much to the annoyance of the Fed, which wishes less attention were paid to the weekly fluctuations). And you expect them to believe that a huge jump is okay because of some behavioral "phenomenon?"

"Try to explain it to somebody who thinks that the perpetual mistake of the Federal Reserve has been being too easy all the time," Volcker says, "and all he'll say is, well, this is just another rationale for being too easy. And there's always the danger that that is the case. So you've got to be a little cautious about it.

"I suppose we've compromised. We've been restrictive, but not nearly as restrictive as we would have been if we didn't think this phenomenon was occurring."

THE DEFICIT

Volcker is not one who abhors any deficit (particularly in a recession) or who dreams of paying off the national debt. There

may be times, he says—the recession was not one of them—
when it would be appropriate public policy to pay off some of
the debt, to make more room for private borrowing; but, he
says, "a substantial national debt is not a problem. In the context of a huge economy, it's supportable. It's a question of the
speed at which it grows—that's the risk now."

Clearly, it is a risk that became ever more real after our
interview, even as the economy was otherwise blazing ahead.

Although in some senses overblown, the deficit problem is
real. One of the thorniest parts of the deficit problem, in fact, is
that you *have to* overblow its importance. How else to force
any painful action? Yet that, in and of itself, shakes confidence;
shaken confidence crimps the economy; a crimped economy
widens the deficit.

A $200-billion 1985 deficit—overblown? How can anything
so horrendous be overblown? Well, note these mitigating fac-
tors:

1. An economy growing more rapidly than forecast may trim
deficit estimates.

2. When state and local government *surpluses* are added in,
the total government deficit, at 5 or 6 percent of GNP, shrinks
to 3 or 3½ percent. (Admittedly, we could talk a while about
"off-balance sheet financing," another side of that coin.)

3. Gargantuan as the total debt is, at $1.5 trillion, even more
gargantuan are the total financial and physical assets of the
nation, which economist David Bostian estimates exceed $20
trillion.

4. *This* deficit, as Bostian has also pointed out, in no small
measure results from tax breaks given business to modernize
and expand. To that extent, it is borrowing to invest rather than
to consume, and should one day bear fruit.

5. Part of the deficit problem is self-fulfilling. Because it is
high, the market keeps interest rates high; when it is perceived

to be narrowing, interest rates will fall—and that will narrow the deficit still further.

6. Most importantly, the deficit *can* be narrowed—and a national consensus appears to be building to narrow it. At some point the growth in defense spending *will* be cut (at no great sacrifice). At some point the adjustments by which Social Security payments and income-tax brackets are indexed to rise with inflation could be revised to rise in pace with inflation *minus 3 percent*. (After all, because of statistical imperfections, the rise in Social Security benefits from 1978 through 1982 substantially *exceeded* the rise in the cost of living.) Such a "CPI-minus-3" formula—by no means original with me—would be painful to Social recipients and to taxpayers (would it really be all *that* painful?)—but the Congressional Budget Office has estimated that, alone, it could trim the deficit by $200 billion from 1985 through 1989. That would be (in the words of *The Wall Street Journal*) "a hefty chunk of the $300 billion to $600 billion in deficit reduction measures that many economists estimate will be needed" over those years. Just by passing a really-not-so-terrible law.

I don't say this will be easy, just that it's possible. Perhaps we'll fail. Congress has never been famous for cutting budgets. And it is cutting budgets more than raising taxes that will productively narrow the deficit. Tax hikes, because they dampen economic activity, never seem actually to raise tax revenues.

"I remain convinced," Senate Banking Committee chairman Jake Garn was saying back in the summer of 1982, "that it is the Congress that is primarily to blame for the failure of interest rates to decline as quickly as inflation."

"There is a great effort by Congress," he told Volcker, "to pass the buck to you. You are one of the favorite topics of speeches by congressmen and senators of both parties: 'If only we could get that damn Paul Volcker to do something, all this would go away.' There's never much talk about fiscal policy; never much talk about *our* role in it.

"If we really don't like these budget deficits, why don't we just shut up and do something about it?"

Although it is now voguish for congressmen to rail against the deficit, quite a number in 1982 were incensed at the Fed's intransigence. They were priming the Treasury to borrow half a trillion or more to finance the deficit of the coming three years, and just didn't understand why the average investor, in the face of this, was not willing to accept 4 or 6 or 8 percent on a long-term bond, the way he always used to.

Senator Kennedy walked in near the end of a session at which Volcker was present that summer and began decrying the Fed's independence. "If you were up here as a member of the Treasury," he glowered, "our relationship would be different." Responded Volcker calmly: "That's probably true, but I believe it was intentionally designed this way."

A democracy is better suited to divvying up prosperity than to doling out adversity. Not himself having to run for election, the chairman of the Federal Reserve is able to apply discipline politicians can't or won't.

Does Volcker ever feel incredible frustration that congressmen, for selfish political reasons, are letting the country go down the tubes? That there are answers to a lot of our problems —not easy ones, but not so horribly painful, either—but that rather than face the problems and deal with them logically, even at the risk of losing elections, congressmen would rather risk disaster? Especially if they can blame the other party? Does politics drive Volcker crazy?

The chairman's eyes widen at the notion he would even consider answering a question like that. "You're leaving on the microphone?" he asks; then answers only, "Elections obviously don't make things any easier."

His view of the budget compromises that were sorting their

way through Congress that summer was hopeful but realistic. "It's probably past the time when you could have had a sharp impact on psychology, back when we were looking for a bipartisan [bold stroke]."

Instead you had this sort of report (the *Wall Street Journal,* August 4, 1982): "In a partisan showdown vote, the House refused to limit to 4% the annual cost-of-living increase in civil service retirees' pay, as called for in the fiscal 1983 budget. The Democrat-led House, which had balked at placing the unpopular ceiling on federal pensions in this election year, managed to put Republicans into the uncomfortable position of having to propose the limit without Democratic support if they wanted it passed. The Republicans refused."

WHAT'S SO TERRIBLE
ABOUT A LITTLE INFLATION?

The doomsayers know exactly how this goes. Inflation heats up, so monetary policy tightens. But that becomes painful, so political pressure is brought to bear and, rather than follow through, the Fed turns on the gas. That brings on worse inflation, followed by even more painful tightening, followed by hyperinflation, followed by complete collapse. It's not certain how many cycles this takes, or which one we're in, but in the summer of 1982—and in 1984 as well—the doomsayers were convinced that the only way out of the recession was to plant the seeds of a new inflation—that the public would forget how much it hated inflation and effectively demand it. After all, what's really so terrible about a little inflation?

"More and more people will probably be saying that!" Volcker agreed. But inflation, he explained, is not the harmless little phenomenon it once was. It goes to the very roots of trust in government and society.

"You know," he says, "I grew up, was educated in the period when advanced thinkers said a little bit of inflation was a good thing. People thought they were a little richer each year, the profits were always a little higher than expected, it's *nice* to have the price of your house going up—and, the argument ran, all that will lead to a good economy.

"In fact, I think there is some truth to that, but it's got a big catch: there's only some truth to it so long as people are 'surprised,' implicitly or explicitly, by the inflation." They must not be aware of what's going on. "Once they begin getting the sense that it's a game, and they're just trying to keep ahead of it but can't, then you've got an entirely different set of circumstances.

"I think that is the watershed we passed in the seventies. You could make that earlier argument maybe as late as the midseventies—although it was getting pretty thin even in the early seventies. By the late seventies you could no longer argue it, until by '79 and '80 and now, I would say people are exaggerating in their behavior the degree of inflation we're going to have. They're not willing to take a chance—what appears to them as taking a chance—on stability."

THE PATIENT COULD PULL THROUGH

Through most of the summer of '82, the nation was having a severe—well-founded—anxiety attack. "I believe we have a desperate situation on our hands," an agitated Senator Don Riegle told Volcker at a hearing in July.

It is in that context that Volcker is asked: "Can we get out of this economic box? And in time, say, to save the S&Ls?" The S&Ls, after all, were paying 15 percent and more for money they had lent out in 9 percent mortgages. You can't stay in business too long doing that!

Volcker answers in a way that suggests he knows this box very, very well. (A final match bounces out of the ashtray. As

an experiment, the interviewer decides to sit pat. Is the chairman oblivious to the real world as some of his critics charge?
Slowly, he leans forward, reaches out a long arm and retrieves
the match.)

"Well," he says, "you're asking the question, I guess, how
big the box is. Or how long the box is. There are elements of
that box. The box is certainly longer or tougher, or pieces of
the box are stronger, than you would hope. I think we're about
to get out of the box, in some sense—but that's a projection.

"I don't expect anything very exuberant—and I wouldn't
want anything too exuberant, because sustainability is very important—but you get some recovery going for a while and at
the same time you get interest rates going down, and you get
the inflation rate continuing to go down: I think things begin
interacting in a *nice* way.

"And if you could restrain a recovery and have the inflation
rate continue to fall—and the inflation rate did fall in the last
recovery for a year or so—then you have a quite different set-
ting. Suppose the inflation rate is falling for two or three years
and suppose by that time you're back to something that people
are willing to live with. Then you've won the game in some
sense.

"That's all I'm saying: that some day the *good* scenario
ought to feed upon itself. So the question you're raising, I think,
is how long does the bad scenario feed upon itself before it gets
overtaken by the good one. I hope we're pretty close to that
point! And I think we are. But of course I can't prove it."

A few months before he made these rather prescient com-
ments, the chairman was going to dinner with his wife. (Barbara
Volcker does bookkeeping for an architectural firm in New
York. He usually flies up on weekends to the Manhattan co-op
they bought in 1975 "when everybody thought New York was
going to go bust." Sometimes she comes to stay in the modest
one-bedroom apartment he rents within walking distance of the

Fed.) He went out and got into the car, behind its Federal Reserve driver. "I look over his shoulder"—Volcker enjoys telling this story—"and he's reading a book. The name of the book was: *How to Make Inflation Pay*. I don't know who it was written by, but it was one of those books. Two or three months earlier, you know, we had had a string of good price statistics, and I keep making speeches about things are gonna get better and there he is reading this book! *How to Make Inflation Pay for You*.

"I said, 'Mr. Pina—how can you be reading that book?' He says, 'I was in a bookstore the other day and I saw it marked down from $10.95 to $1.98.' "

A small sign, but a sign.

And as we all know, two years after gridlock, in 1984, inflation was a relatively tame 4 percent. Unemployment was down, production was up—but there were fears. Any number of newsletters saw inflation exploding, gold rising to $3,000 or $4,000 an ounce by 1986, and a boom ahead for subscriptions. Would third world insolvencies force the Fed to print untold tens of billions to rescue the banks? Would growth in the deficit continue to accelerate (which in turn would aggravate inflation and interest rates, which aggravate the deficit)?

After all, 1984 is an election year. Is it time for the old election-year pump-priming as usual? Volcker says no, of course. But does he mean it? Does he really, really mean it?

To give in now, the second most powerful man in America tells audiences whenever his resolve is questioned, could only greatly complicate matters over the long run. "It would strike me as the cruelest blow of all," he says, "to the millions who have felt the pain of the recession to suggest, in effect, it was all in vain."

Listening, it's hard to resist the temptation to put at least some of one's money, should one be so lucky as to have some money (the chairman's own net worth, exclusive of his apartment, is listed at $56,000), into long-term bonds.

GLOSSARY

Terms of Enrichment

The entries that follow are arranged alphalogibetically:

Annual Reports. Like parents' day at camp. Everything is made to look as appealing as possible, but the counselors know different.

If you are going to read them, start from the back. Read the auditor's opinion first (beware the words "except for" and "subject to"), footnotes second (beware those that seem deliberately incomprehensible), financial statements third (beware parentheses; they indicate losses) and only then the illustrated narrative in the front.

But as you won't be able to analyze the report any better than a pro—who got all this info months ago—why bother? Go out and play like the other kids.

Bonds. When *you* borrow money it's called an auto loan. When GM borrows money it's called a bond issue. Bonds are nothing more than i.o.u.'s. They are issued with "face values" of $1,000. Their "coupon rates" are the annual interest they pay (although it is paid semiannually). If a $1,000 GM bond with an 8 percent coupon is "76¼ bid," that means (a) it pays $40 every six months and (b) even though it will be redeemed for $1,000 at maturity, all you can get for it today is 76¼ cents on the dollar ($762.50).

Bearer Bonds. Bearer bonds are not issued in your name— they are unregistered—so anyone who shows up bearing them (as in "Damn, dese bonds is heavy!") is presumed to own them. However, rather than make you show up with the bonds every six months, bond issuers append coupons to the certificates—forty of them in the case of a twenty year bond—so that you can just clip the proper coupon and deposit it with your bank. Some people still clip coupons, but most entrust their holdings to their brokers and leave the coupon clipping to a computer.

Borrowing. The only way you can make money borrowing at 14 percent is if you have a way to invest that money at *15 percent*. This is a notion few seem to grasp.

True, interest is tax deductible and capital appreciation, partially tax-free. And a lot of money has been made—or at least spared from tax—on the difference. But borrowing at 14 percent (pretax) in hope of, say, 11 percent (after tax) is a risky way to get rich.

Bankruptcy. A way to steal from society without serious penalty. Lots of people advertise how painless and advantageous it is (it's advantageous for them; they get a fee).

Bankruptcy resulting from catastrophic illness or some similar calamity is a different matter, morally valid. But that's not what the ads are about.

Bucket Shops. In colonial days, these were located mostly in suburban shopping malls and sold nothing but buckets, barrels and—in the larger malls—vats. Nowadays, bucket shops are located in large rooms on low floors of Florida and Oklahoma office buildings and sell, by phone, commodity options, oil-lease lottery tickets and penny mining shares. If a guy calls you on the phone and offers to send an illustrated brochure promising Great Wealth, by all means accept! And then send him your $5,000, even though he's a total stranger who's reading his sales pitch from a script, because *this could be your lucky day*. This could be the one such offer in all of recorded time that works out just the way the salesman says it will.

Big Board. Not to be confused with Big Bird or bed board: the august New York Stock Exchange.

The Amex. Should by rights be known as the Little Board, but is actually known as the Curb: the American Stock Exchange. (Not to be confused with AMEX, short for: Shearson-Lehman - Bros. - Kuhn - Loeb - Hayden - Stone - IDS - Fireman's-Fund - Boston - Company - Balcor - Safra - Robinson - Humphrey/ American Express.)

OTC. Over-the-Counter. Stocks not traded on one of the major exchanges (or the Pacific, Boston, Philadelphia or Midwest exchangelets) are traded by "market-makers," linked by phones and computers, "over-the-counter." Not to be confused with GTC, which is short for "good till canceled" (as when your broker asks, "Is this order to buy 1,000 Orfa at 2½ for the day only or good till canceled?").

NASDAQ. The National Association of Securities Dealers Automated Quotation system. Over-the-counter stocks aren't traded on an exchange, but thousands of them are "on NASDAQ," meaning that your broker can punch their symbols into the terminal on his desk and tell you, "It's one-and-an-eighth bid, but our people are confident it'll come back."

Capital Gains. You buy something, then sell it for more. The difference is a capital gain. (Unless you are in *business* to buy and sell it, like bras or steel tubing. Then the difference, net of expenses, is called income.) There are short-term gains and long-term gains, depending on whether you owned the stock or

bond or horse or house more than six months (twelve months
for assets purchased before June 23, 1984). Currently, 60 percent of a long-term gain is exempt from tax. See also: ILL-
GOTTEN GAINS.

Capital Losses. You buy something, then sell it for *less*. The
difference should teach you a lesson but probably won't. Up to
$3,000 of short-term losses may be deducted, dollar for dollar,
from your ordinary income, with the remainder carried forward
to future years. But only half your long-term losses are deductible. See also: LOWER-CASE LOSSES.

Basis. The amount on which your gain or loss is figured.
Ordinarily, it is your purchase price. But what if you inherited
the asset? (These days, your basis would be its appraised value
as of the date of death.) Or depreciated it? (Your basis is low-
ered by the amount of depreciation.) Or improved it? (Your
basis is increased by the cost of the improvements.) The second
year of law school is devoted entirely to this paragraph.

Common Stocks. The foundation of the economy, the source
of corporate capital; also known as "equities." Shares of stock
represent shares of corporate ownership—although management frequently tends to forget this.

Debt and Equity. The typical company will be funded with
two kinds of capital. Money the owners paid in to get the business going (along with profits they decided to leave in to help
the business grow)—called equity. And borrowed money that
must some day be paid back—debt.

A firm's "debt-to-equity" ratio is thus a fundamental measure of its solidity. A firm that has $20 million in debt and $10
million in equity (a nerve-chilling 2-to-1 ratio) is far less solid,
other things being equal, than one with $5 million in debt and
$25 million in equity (a debt/equity ratio of .2).

Bid and Asked. Ask for a price and you get a question: *Are you buying or selling?* A stock or bond that's "74, 76" is "$74 bid, $76 asked." I'm trying to find a country where that means you can buy it for $74 or sell it for $76, but so far, every place I've been, it works the other way around. Maybe Bulgaria.

Long and Short. If you own 150 shares of GM, you are "long GM." If you've sold 150 shares of GM you don't own (and will thus some day have to buy back), you are "short GM."

When you short a stock, you borrow it from your broker in order to sell it. You get none of the *cash* for selling it (the broker keeps that, plus the interest it earns), but you do make a profit if, when you go to buy it back, it costs less than what you paid. There's no time limit within which you must return the stock to your broker—it's not like a library book—and in fact the longer you're short, the happier the broker is, because he's earning interest on the proceeds of your sale. Currently, with about 200 million shares short, at perhaps $25 each, the brokerage community is earning interest on $5 billion in customer short sales, and passing on not a penny of it to its customers (except to a scant few powerful ones who have the muscle to demand it). I realize this is much more than you ever wanted to know about the subject, but it accounts for half a billion dollars a year in profit to Wall Street so I'm telling you anyway.

Now. If the stock you're short pays a dividend, you don't get it—you *pay* it. Your broker slips that cash into the account of the true owner of the shares you borrowed, who will never even know they're gone. (Should *he* wish to sell his shares before you've returned them, the broker quick like a bunny borrows them from someone else.)

You can't short everything, but you can short a lot: cotton, pork bellies, the yen, many stocks, all publicly traded commodities and currencies and options. To do so successfully takes luck and courage that borders on the witless. Some very tall people are short, but, with time, get cut down to size.

Puts and Calls. These are options to buy or sell shares of stock. They are not unlike the red and black lines at roulette, only at roulette your odds of winning are better and you get free drinks.

You buy a call on GM if you expect it to go up; a put if you expect it to go down. You can also *sell* a call instead of buying a put, or sell a put instead of buying a call, or buy and sell a couple of each to set up spreads and straddles, but all this means is that you're really getting hooked in a way that can ultimately profit only your broker.

Debentures. Bonds.

Convertible Bonds. Bonds that have an "equity kicker"— namely, they can be traded in for a set number of shares of stock. For example, Pan Am has a 15 percent convertible bond that promises to pay $1,000 at maturity, but that once sold for $1,600. Why? Because part of the deal is that you can convert it into 182 shares of Pan Am common stock, then worth over $8 apiece.

Municipal Bonds. Issued by local governments and county sewage authorities, they are free of federal (and their own state) tax. As has been pointed out ad nauseum: to someone in the 50 percent tax bracket a 9 percent tax-free bond is equivalent to an 18 percent taxable one.

Call Features. Many bonds are "callable" after just a few years. That gives the issuer the right to redeem them years in advance of maturity, just as you have the right to prepay your mortgage. Most recently issued municipal bonds don't mature for twenty years or more but are callable in ten.

Preferred Stocks. Like bonds that *never* mature (but that in some cases are callable). These shares pay a dividend that never goes up, no matter how prosperous the company, but that won't go down, either, unless things get really bad. Most are "cumulative" preferreds, meaning that if dividends *are* omitted they must all be paid before a nickel can be paid out to the common shareholders. Some preferreds are "convertible," too.

Corporations like to buy preferred stocks because for corporations dividends are 85 percent tax-free.

Commercial Paper. Short-term corporate i.o.u.'s backed by nothing more than a big company's promise to repay. These have nothing to do with you or me. They come in denominations like $1 million and are placed with the Big Guys.

Diversification. Eggs, baskets . . . you know.

Dividends. There are two problems with dividends. They are relatively small and they are fully taxed. Real men don't dream of dividends, they dream of doubling their money overnight. That is why real men have these great craggy jaws and hyper-masculine footwear but little in the way of financial security.

Stock Dividends. These are what a company pays when it can't afford to pay cash. No tax is due on them, because they are entirely worthless. Previously there was a pie that was split up into a lot of little slices. Now there is exactly the same pie, only it is split up into slightly smaller pieces. Management hopes you will be too stupid to realize this.

Dividend Reinvestment Plans. This is different. Here, you opt to use your real dividends to buy more shares. You do have to pay taxes (except in the case of utility stocks, many of which afford a tax break—ask your broker).

Earnings. The preferred word for a company's profits. And what are profits? The sum of all the positive bookkeeping entries, many of which may have nothing to do with real cash coming in the door (such as: sales that have been made but not paid for), less all the negative entries, many of which—that's right—may have nothing to do with real cash going *out* the door (such as: taxes that would have had to be paid if we hadn't found a way to defer them).

Cash Flow. In many respects more important than earnings, this is the simpleminded measure of how much cash is pouring in or draining out. Real estate operations always report bad earnings (because of the depreciation they claim, for tax purposes, on their properties), but the cash just rolls in bigger and bigger each year (because the properties actually *ap*preciate and the rents get raised).

Earnings Per Share. All the earnings divided by all the shares.

Retained Earnings. The portion of earnings *not* paid out to shareholders in dividends. Sometimes this money is retained by the company for expansion and reinvestment, and sometimes it is retained because it exists only on paper. (Sometimes it exists only on paper but is paid out anyway, by going deeper into hock.)

Float. Because money has "time value," it's great to have someone else's, even for a little while, without having to pay interest on it. When you charge something on your American Express card, you have use of American Express's money until (a) they bill you, which takes a while; (b) you pay them, which takes a while longer; (c) your check clears, which takes a while longer still. This is "the float," and one reason American Express has 16 million fans. But American Express understands float, too. (How's that for understatement?) All those travelers' checks we buy are interest-free cash in Amex's pocket until they're redeemed.

Futures. One of the few ways in life to lose more than you bet. You put up only $2,000 to control 15,000 pounds of frozen orange juice worth $22,500. Your hope is not to take delivery of the juice when it's due at a specified date in the future—your freezer is already packed to overflowing, and you prefer fresh-squeezed anyway—but to sell it at a profit to someone else. If your juice, worth $22,500 when you bought it, goes to $24,500, you've doubled your $2,000 (less commissions and taxes). If it falls to $16,000, you're screwed. You lose not just the $2,000, but another $4,500 and commissions besides. There are commodity futures and currency futures. To be certain of losing only what you invest, but no more, you can now buy *options* on futures.

Go Public. The modern equivalent of "strike gold." Namely, when a privately held company first offers stock to the public.

Gold. If you expect virulent inflation, buy some. Better still, buy silver.

GTC. If you were paying attention (see OTC, above), you already know that this means "good till canceled." But brokers say it means "good till close." You put in your order to buy 1,000 Pan Am at 5, good-till-canceled, should it ever go so low. For months that order sits on the books. But when Pan Am gets down close to 5, around 5⅜, you begin to get very nervous (maybe there's a *reason* it's dropped so low!) and you call your broker and say, "You know that order I have in on Pan Am?" And before you can say another word, he begins writing up the ticket to cancel the order.

Interest Rates. When they're headed up, everything else goes down and infants whimper in their cribs (it's instinctual). When they're headed down, everything else goes up and it's as if a box of David's Cookies had just been delivered to every family's door.

Investing. Taking your savings out of the bank (because you think only plodders keep their money in banks) and placing it at greater risk. When interest rates are headed down, you'll do well. When they're headed up, you'll do poorly. If you get to thinking you can psych out which way they're headed, you'll be sorry.

IRAs, Keoghs, Salary Reduction Plans. Personal pension funds, the tax shelter for Little Guys. Can't be recommended highly enough.

JNL. One of several all but incomprehensible abbreviations on brokerage statements. Short for "Journal," it means, "This is a journal entry only. It didn't really happen. We're not completely clear on what it means, either." Other common abbreviations include FDS (funds), TFR (transfer, as in the fds that are forever being mysteriously tfrd from your tpl acct to your tp6 acct and then jnld to tp2), ADJ (adjustment, which means "We screwed up") and UNC FDS (uncollected funds, which means *you* screwed up by sending in a rubber check).

K-1. See "Limited Partnership," below. Not to be confused with 10K's, which companies must file with the SEC each year (the *real* annual report) or 10Q's, which they must file quarterly. Nor 13D's, which must be filed if they acquire 5 percent or more of another company's shares. Nor 10b-5, the rule under which those who trade on inside information get their bones crushed.

Letter Stock. This is stock that comes with special rules attached and, hey, it's great stuff. Nationwide Nursing Centers is selling in the open market at $22 a share; one of the founders is hot to sell 200,000 shares. The SEC restricts the sale of "unregistered" shares, but allows them to be placed privately. So Nationwide (how fly-by-night could they be if they're nationwide?) offers it to you at $8. The only catch is that it's "letter stock," also known as restricted stock, and there's a big fat paragraph on the back of the certificate that says you've got to wait two years before you sell so much as a single share or the SEC will cut your balls off. Two years is a long time to wait with a stock like Nationwide Nursing Centers.

Leverage and Hedging. Leverage is a way to increase risk—and reward—usually through the use of debt. If you buy a $100,000 house for cash and it appreciates $10,000, you've made 10 percent on your money. If you buy the same house with $5,000 down and it appreciates $10,000, you've made *200 percent* on your money (assuming your tenants pay enough to cover your carrying costs—a big assumption these days).

Hedging is a way to *reduce* risk. If you buy 100 shares of GM, hoping it will go up, you can hedge your bet by buying a put on GM shares, in case they go down. It always costs something to hedge—usually too much—but sometimes it's worth it. Like insurance. The cheapest way to hedge is simply to diversify. (See DIVERSIFICATION, above.)

Leveraged Buy-outs. Here you and your buddies pool $50,000 in hard cash and make a bid to take over Time, Inc. You do that by borrowing three or four billion dollars from a large bank on the understanding that the minute you've bought the company you will use its own cash and underutilized borrowing power to secure the loan, and if that's not enough, you'll sell *Sports Illustrated* and your summer house.

Sounds crazy, I know. But in our little village of Anatevka . . .

Limited Partnership. An entity through which to give up all control over your money in hope of great gain. You may invest in as many of these deals as you like—both the private kind, often limited to just thirty-five investors, and the public kind, which come to you from All the Major Firms—and they entitle you, if nothing else, to a K-1 shortly after the end of the year. The K-1 documents your share of the partnership's income or loss, which you then report on Schedule E. The K-1 is promised to arrive no later than March 15 to give you time to file your taxes. In fact, it generally arrives April 14, late in the afternoon. (See also, TAX SHELTERS.)

Liquidity. Cash is liquid. Stocks and bonds are liquid, too: you can sell them and have cash in a week. Real estate is illiquid (it takes a while to sell), but not nearly so illiquid as many limited partnership units, which you can be stuck with for years and years and years. Wine, strangely enough, is only semi-liquid.

Millionaire. Someone worth $5 million or more. (Let's be realistic.)

Margin. You can buy securities for cash, or you can buy them "on margin." The Federal Reserve sets the minimum down payment, currently 50 percent for stocks. The rest of the purchase price is loaned to you by your broker, at no risk (to him) but considerable profit.

Bonds may be purchased on even thinner margin and Treasury securities on thinnest of all.

Should your stocks or bonds or Treasuries decline in value, you will begin getting urgent Mailgrams long before your equity is wiped out. If you don't send more cash or instruct your broker to sell something, your broker will take it upon himself to sell something for you.

OPM. "Other people's money." As in, "the secret of business is never to put any of your own money on the line—do the deal with OPM. If it works out, you've got a fat share of the profit for putting it together; if it bombs, well, the investors knew it was risky." OPM is particularly useful to entrepreneurs who have no M of their own.

Pink Sheets. The *Wall Street Journal* lists lots of stocks and bonds, but by no means all of them. If you ask your broker for a price on some ridiculous little number you heard about on the golf course, he will yell, "Harry! You got the pink sheets over there?" And Harry will toss over a stapled sheaf of thin pink paper crammed with bid-and-asked prices for the stocks of a zillion little companies. The yellow sheets are for obscure corporate bonds; the blue sheets, for municipal bonds (virtually all of which are obscure).

Par. A bond that sells at par sells at 100 cents on the dollar, which is to say its full $1,000 face value.

Par Value. With a bond, $1,000. With a common stock, meaningless.

P/E. A stock's p/e is its "price/earnings ratio" or "multiple." If a stock "earns" $4.40 a share and sells for $45, it is selling for a tad above ten times earnings. Its p/e is 10.2. Of course, it's *next* year's earnings that are most interesting, not last year's . . . but that's not the basis of the p/e you'll find listed in the paper.

Present Value. A dollar today is worth more than the promise of a dollar a year from now, even if you're absolutely certain that promise will be fulfilled. ("Hey, the guy's never screwed me before!") That's because of "the time value of money": namely, what you can do with it in the meantime. If you can earn 11 percent interest on your dollar in a year, then, really, a dollar a year from now is worth only about 90 cents now—its present value. Why? Because 90 cents will grow to a dollar a year from now.

The present value of $236,981.34 eight-and-a-half years from now is a slightly more complicated calculation, but the very same idea. The present value all depends on the "discount rate" you choose. Above, we chose 11 percent, because that's what we thought money could earn in a year. The higher the rate you assume, the less future money is worth today. And vice versa.

The entire first year of business school is devoted to this concept.

Precious Metals. Some are more precious than others and all are less precious than they were when the world was about to end in January 1980.

Strategic Metals. These include chromium, germanium, iridium, titanium, vanadium, zirconium, ruthenium and columbiam, among others, and were the subject of a brief flurry of speculative attention at around the same time. Lithium is the only one you should ever even consider, and then only on the advice of your physician.

Mutual Fund. Takes your cash and everybody else's and invests more or less as advertised. Some invest aggressively for capital gains (and get mauled in a bear market), some invest mostly in foreign stocks or gold stocks or technology stocks or high-grade bonds or low-grade bonds or "a diversified portfolio of seasoned equities balanced so as to provide meaningful income while seeking to enhance values through capital appreciation." (The big money, let's face it, is in writing brochures.)

All mutual funds charge a modest management fee, but some charge a one-time sales fee, as well. Called the load, it is often as high as 8.5 percent of your investment. Ordinarily, you will want to stick to "no-load" funds.

Money Market Fund. A mutual fund designed to be a cross between a savings account and a checking account. It invests mostly in short-term government and corporate securities, for liquidity, safety and yield.

Sinking Fund. A mutual fund that attracts so much money from the public that it sinks beneath the waves under the weight. "Off-shore" sinking funds are thus particularly dangerous.

No, wait. That's *stinking* fund.

Sinking Fund. GM sells $100 million in twenty-year bonds (say) and one of the provisions of the bond is that GM must set up a sinking fund to redeem a certain portion of the bonds each year. A trustee is engaged to pull numbers out of a hat to see whose bonds get redeemed. This is a lottery one generally hopes not to win.

Prospectus. A fat legal document you will not read, filled with warnings, risks and disclosures you will ignore, that must accompany the issuance of any new security.

Proxy Statements. Usually accompany annual reports and are your chance to vote the current board of directors out of office and elect a board composed entirely of goblins and elves. All you need is another 48 million shares.

Prudence. Prudence, though boring, is an attribute earnestly to be sought. It is not to be confused with the stodginess or poverty of intellect associated with certain bank trust departments.

Quarterly Reports. Like annual reports only shorter and unaudited. Meaning that the numbers are even more fanciful.

Red Herring. A rough-draft prospectus, before the final numbers have been filled in and the SEC go-ahead obtained.

Saving. A terrific habit, less easily formed than most others.

Scripophily. Pronounced scri-PAH-fil-ee, it is the collection of worthless old stock and bond certificates like the one I have from Nationwide Nursing Centers.

Speculating. Selling your shares in Ford—which only tripled in the last couple of years—to try for some really *big* bucks. It's true that Truman had a sign on his desk that said THE BUCK STOPS HERE. What's less well known is that he swiped it from his broker.

Stop Loss. You enter a stop loss order "at 18" so that if the stock you bought at 20 drops to 3, you won't lose everything—just the two points between 20 and 18. Your stock will be sold automatically if it drops to 18. This is especially good if you go off into the bush for a few weeks and the battery in your port-a-phone goes dead. It is also recommended by many pros as a means of disciplining yourself to "cut your losses" while "letting your profits run."

There are two problems with this. First, it means you're likely to get whipsawed a lot. Say a stock is down from 40 to 22 and you think it's really a good value. But to be safe, you put in a stop at 19½ when you buy it. The market takes a dive, the stock drops to 19, you're stopped out at 19½, and then it bounces back to 22 and begins a steady climb to 40. The pro will say, "Okay, that can happen; but if you set tight stops, you can never lose more than 10 or 15 percent on a stock." True, but you could lose it over and over again, and it begins to mount up. If the stock was a good buy at 22, might it not be even better at 19½? The pro will tell you that stops protect you against problems within the company your research failed to turn up. (If the stock is headed down, maybe the sellers know more than you do.) And on that score, the pro is right.

The second problem is that placing a stop at 19½ only guarantees you'll get out at that price if the drop in the stock is gradual. If, instead, it's revealed that the six top executives of this company (a major defense contractor) are Soviet agents, the stock—22 yesterday—could open for trading at 8⅝ today. You won't get 19½, you'll get 8⅝. (And if the stock then bounces back to 13 by noon, you may wish you'd been consulted.)

Tax Avoidance. Perfectly legal, or quasi-legal, attempts to slip through the cracks of the law and shift the burden of taxation to your neighbor.

Tax Evasion. Things like failure to report income or the fabrication of phony deductions. Out-and-out fraud.

Tax Shelter. A means of paying a dollar to avoid paying 50 cents in taxes. Many billions of dollars are raised for this purpose every year, of which at least 15 or 20 percent is typically skimmed off the top by the promoters, lawyers and salespeople.

Technical Analysis. Trying to guess where prices are headed by looking at where they've been. As opposed to "fundamental analysis." A technical analyst might say, "Silver looks very strong; it's just pierced its 120-day moving average." A fundamental analyst would say, "Silver looks very strong; demand in both the photographic and electrical connector markets is picking up with no corresponding increase in production." A technical analyst might say, "Apple's chart looks terrific." A fundamental analyst would say, "I'm impressed by the marketing skills of the new president and the potential appeal of the products in the pipeline.''

Teenies. When a stock is quoted 3³⁄₁₆ you don't say, "three and three-sixteenths," you say "three and three steenths." Or, "three and three teenies."

Tender Offers. These are tender only when they are "friendly." An unfriendly tender offer is one in which Boone Pickens of Mesa Petroleum is trying to get you to tender (sell) your shares in some giant oil company to him at a fat price, and the management of that giant oil company is doing everything it possibly can to save its jobs and keep you from getting that fat price.

Ticks. Every time a stock trades, it's a tick. The stream of all these trades is recorded on the ticker tape, which is now almost entirely electronic, no longer makes a tick-e-ta-tick-et-a sound, and could cause a problem the next time we win a war and try to stage a ticker tape parade. There are two kinds of ticks: upticks, if the last different price at which the stock in question traded was lower; and downticks, if the last different price was higher. (A stock could trade fifty times in a row at 23, but if the last different price was 22⅞, all fifty of those trades at 23 are upticks.) You may only short a stock on an uptick. This rule is meant to keep short-selling from compounding the severity of regular selling. There is no such thing as a tock.

Ticket. You'd think a brokerage ticket is something your broker gives you when you leave a stock or bond with him for safekeeping, like a coat check. Actually, it's the form he uses to write up an order.

Unit. What Texans call $100 million. As in, "Oh, Bucky? He's got a couple of units."

Upside Potential, Downside Risk. This is what people who can't speak English call "potential" and "risk."

U.S. Savings Bonds. Still a great gift for a baby, and not as bad a deal as they once were, especially for the small saver.

Would'a Could'a Should'a. What brokers hear all day from their customers. "I should'a shorted the son of a bitch! If I'd'a shorted a thousand shares, I could'a made—what?—twenty grand in a week!"

X. This is the symbol for US Steel, which is now primarily an oil company. XON is the symbol for *the* primary oil company. XRX is Xerox, IBM is IBM, JOB is General Employment Enterprises, EYE is Coopervision, BTU is Pyro Energy and AMTC is Nature's Sunshine Products. (Some symbols are more immediately memorable than others.) Any that have more than three letters are for stocks traded over the counter.

Yield. The income an investment throws off, be it interest or dividend, is its yield. An 8 percent bond selling at 80 "yields" 10 percent. (If it were selling at par, it would yield 8 percent.)

Zero Coupon Bonds. They pay no interest but don't cost a lot, either. And one day they'll be redeemed for $1,000 apiece. A great way to start an IRA. Currently, $2,000 will buy $24,000 of CATS maturing in 2012. (Your broker will know what they are.)

Index

ABOUT THE AUTHOR

ANDREW TOBIAS, a graduate of Harvard College and Harvard Business School, was born in New York in 1947 and is the author of several books, including three national best sellers: *Fire and Ice, The Only Investment Guide You'll Ever Need,* and *The Invisible Bankers.* He is the winner of the 1984 Gerald Loeb Award for distinguished business and financial journalism, and is the author, as well, of *Managing Your Money,* a computer software package that *Personal Software* called "Simply the finest personal financial management program on the market."